GOLF FOR WOMEN

by

LOUISE SUGGS

and

MARLENE BAUER HAGGE

BEVERLY HANSON

JACKIE PUNG

BARBARA ROMACK

JOYCE ZISKE

RUTH JESSEN

CORNERSTONE LIBRARY   **NEW YORK**

editor in chief fred r. sammis
supervising editor louise suggs
editor pat hagan murray
art director philip ciminelli

Louise Suggs, Marlene Bauer Hagge, Beverly Hanson, Jackie Pung, Barbara Romack, Joyce Ziske and Ruth Jessen are members of the advisory staff of The MacGregor Co. of Cincinnati, Ohio.

The amateur players appearing in *The Practice Tee* sections are: Ruth Davis, Pamela G. Dawsey, Erma Freeman, Kelly Fuller, Jane Steerman Johnson, Peggy Lynch, Mary L. Newcomb and Martha M. Owen.

The questions asked in the chapter *The Golf Clinic* were compiled with the help of Mike Chiapetta, Wee Burn Country Club professional, and Angie Manero, Darien Driving Range professional.

Practice Tee photographs for Chapters II, IV, V, VII, VIII, IX and X by Howard Modavis; Chapter III by John T. Closs; Chapter VI by Cal Pictures, Inc. Text illustrations by Daniel R. Rubin.

All clothes in Chapter XII courtesy of the David H. Smith Company. Equipment courtesy of The MacGregor Co. Rainwear and golf carts from Abercrombie & Fitch.

CORNERSTONE LIBRARY PUBLICATIONS
ARE DISTRIBUTED BY
AFFILIATED PUBLISHERS
A DIVISION OF POCKET BOOKS, INC.
ROCKEFELLER CENTER
630 FIFTH AVENUE, NEW YORK 20, N.Y.

MANUFACTURED IN THE UNITED STATES OF AMERICA

CONTENTS

Foreword: Tommy Armour 6

Chapter 1
    IT'S ALL IN YOUR HEAD: Louise Suggs 8
Chapter 2
    THE SHORT IRONS: Barbara Romack 20
Chapter 3
    THE MEDIUM IRONS: Ruth Jessen 38
Chapter 4
    THE LONG IRONS: Beverly Hanson 56
Chapter 5
    THE FAIRWAY WOODS: Joyce Ziske 76
Chapter 6
    THE DRIVE: Jackie Pung 96
Chapter 7
    THE APPROACH: Marlene Bauer Hagge 116
Chapter 8
    TRAP SHOTS: Louise Suggs 138
Chapter 9
    TROUBLE SHOTS: Marlene Bauer Hagge 150
Chapter 10
    PUTTING: Louise Suggs 162
Chapter 11
    THE GOLF CLINIC 174
Chapter 12
    CLOTHES FOR THE COURSE: Louise Suggs 182
Chapter 13
    THE RULES AND ETIQUETTE OF GOLF 186

WHAT THIS BOOK IS ABOUT —— AND WHY

GOLF FOR WOMEN is a completely new, completely fresh approach to learning golf. Even the briefest study of its chapters will give the reader a quicker, more accurate grasp of the game's fundamentals—and subtleties— and lead to improved play.

First, all the thoughts — and words — are literally those of the women professionals whose advice makes up this book. A tape recorder on the golf course magnetically imprisoned the precise and permanent record of each chapter.

Second, this is the first time that a group of famous women players have been brought together in the same book, blending their knowledge and tournament experience toward the accomplishment of the common goal of teaching you, the reader.

Third, the instruction chapters begin, not where the conventional golf book begins, but where the actual golf lesson always begins: with the short irons. The driver comes last, where it belongs in the teaching sequence.

Fourth, each chapter is followed by a

Practice Tee lesson. This is a unique modification of actual pro instruction with the best women golfers in the world. It is a wonderfully clear combination of candid photographs and spoken text, taken directly from the tape recorder that was on the tee alongside pro and pupil. In each instance, the pupil is an amateur woman golfer striving for improvement of her game, with skill that ranges from the beginning duffer to the low handicapper. When you read the words and study the photographs, it will be as though you were on the tee yourself, having your own $50 lesson.

The lone male allowed entrance to these pages is the dean of all professional teachers of golf, Tommy Armour. The editor is Louise Suggs, peer of Armour, who, as the dean of all women players, compiled a 1959 tournament-round 18-hole average of 73.8! The reporter-writer whose ability brought together pro, photographer, pupil, and tape recorder, and whose organizational talents brought the whole to this publishing conclusion, is Pat Hagan Murray.

THE PUBLISHERS

FOREWORD BY
TOMMY ARMOUR

It is an honor and a pleasure to be asked to write a foreword to this new and different golf book for the hundreds of thousands of women who are eager to improve their game. The writers who have collaborated in this effort —Mesdames Hagge, Hanson, Pung, Romack, Suggs, Jessen, and Ziske—are, as we all know, celebrated professional golfers. But in addition, they are extremely well-qualified teachers of every aspect of this wonderful and exacting sport.

In my many years of experience, the difference in teaching men and women has always been a great problem. Although both male and female have two legs and two arms, their structures differ, and inescapably men are much stronger and generally have greater athletic ability than women. I have always found it very difficult to adjust myself men-

tally to these differences. And, as I think most pros will tell you, they make golf instruction an extremely difficult task.

Now, when you have collaborators such as the ladies who are writing this book, who have gone through the whole mill of golf from beginner to expert, it must be obvious that they have a great knowledge of the game and all its vagaries and are extremely well-equipped to help women golfers.

When I first heard that this book was being published, I thought it was a project not only constructive, but brilliant. These ladies know the game inside out. I have had the pleasure of discussing and playing golf with some of them, and I can definitely state that they know what they are talking about. This book will undoubtedly be a great boon to women golfers, and I would guess that a number of men could also pick up much valuable information.

It is bound to be a success because it answers both a demand and a great need.

Chapter 1

It's All In Your Head
by Louise Suggs

Women can be better golfers than men!

• Golf has been my life for twenty-six years, so it's not easy for me to be objective about it. By and large, it's been a good life, too, so the prejudices show up more than they might with someone else. But when it comes to this fascinating and frustrating game, there are a few convictions I hold that are based on observation and are not to be classified as prejudices.

One of these convictions has to do with women and golf. There's been far too much of this nonsense, so far as I'm concerned, about women being inferior on the golf course, the people who make this claim usually basing their argument on the female's physical structure. To them I say: "If a woman can walk, she can play golf!"

I'll say also that a woman's golf game *is* different from a man's. A woman—unless she's a Patty Berg, or the late Babe Zaharias—will not be able to slam the ball down the fairway with the power that a Hogan or a Souchak brings to his game. What too many people don't realize, however, is that a woman has a few

9

natural advantages which a man doesn't have when it comes to connecting a club with its white target. One of these advantages is sensitivity—a kind of perception that gets down into her fingertips and comes out when she's holding a putter. She "feels" her game more strongly than a man.

For instance, when somebody asks me how hard I stroke a sixteen-foot putt, I've got to answer, "I don't know. I look at the ball; I look at the cup; I take in the kind of lie I've got. And when I've done that, I just *feel* I've got to hit the ball in a certain way." This "feeling" is the most important factor in a woman's game. Women can birdie a hole on "feel" alone.

Perhaps the first consideration for a woman golfer is the reaction she will suffer from walking into this man's world. She will feel diffident about taking up a game so long dominated by the male sex. There isn't really very much I can say about this. The only mistake I'd caution against is the natural one a woman can make under these circumstances: over-aggression. Play the game as well as you know how and think of the initial breakthrough much as you would if you were moving into a new community. It seems unfriendly— at first. There is resistance—at first. But the opposition will melt before two positive qualities: the ability to play and the grace you would manifest in any social situation.

The most important advice I'd give any woman just starting to play is: get the fundamentals down pat! It's a bad mistake simply to pick up a club and start swinging. If you can afford them, lessons

from a competent pro will be worth their weight in birdies; if money is a consideration, join a group to take lessons.

When the old question, "What is the most important part of the game?" is thrown at me, I don't have to think twice. I answer, "The grip." Without that basic, anyone's form is bound to be way off. From the grip we build to the stance and from the stance we graduate to the heart of the game itself, the swing. These are the imperatives. Without them, one can't achieve even the status of a duffer; with them, one has a game. The rest is merely refinement. I know that this sounds like heresy, but too much has been said and written — mostly by men — about the intricacies of golf, and the theories behind each movement. I suggest that these theories be tossed out the window. While it is a lucky thing for us professionals that most people seem to prefer their golf theories tricked up, it is also a fact that the game is not tricky, or even complicated. I will admit that, to a considerable extent, the movements involved are unnatural movements, but that's as far as the complexity goes. Perhaps a mental picture I've carried around for years may help you.

The golf swing itself, incorporating the fundamentals, is the focal point of the game. And of that swing, including as it does the grip and the stance, the most important feature is the position of the head. So, I think of my head as the hub on a wagon wheel, the position of my arms at the successive stages of the swing as the spokes. That's all. The clubhead will describe that perfect circle. Sometimes it will go all the way, sometimes it won't, but remove that hub (fall away from the ball, jerk the head to one side), and you've lost the smooth rhythm that brings results. To carry my mental picture to its natural conclusion, should the hub go, the wheel will fall off the axle and the wagon itself will break down completely. Now, once this basic movement has been assimilated, it's merely a question of getting the woman's co-ordination to the point where the swing is a natural, rhythmic, one-piece thing. At this point, she has a working game.

Let's retrace. I said that if a woman can walk, she can play golf. I'll elaborate on that a bit. If she's serious about wanting to learn the game, it doesn't make much difference whether her age is 11, 31, or 51. Suppleness is an asset, lack of it a limitation, but a reasonably active woman who takes up the game at 51 will still be able to become a completely competent golfer. Nor will a woman's size make any appreciable difference. To some extent, size will be a factor in the length of her shots, but here again, work on co-ordination can do much to make up for lack of power. Now, I'm aware that there is a vast range and variation in individual co-ordination. There are natural-born athletes, as there are natural-born dancers. But I've seen some men and women, too, who started out with two left feet on the dance floor, and who persevered until they had developed the rhythm necessary for the intricacies of the fox trot. The same thing is true of golf.

A woman who wants to play golf has definite advantages for the development of facility beyond this "feeling" I've mentioned at the beginning. A woman is, in most cases, not only more flexible, but comes very close to being double-jointed. She may never suspect that this is so, but she'll find out in jig-time when she begins working on grip and swing. It is often much easier for her to adapt her body to the rigors of the follow-through, for instance, than it is for her more muscular and power-conscious husband.

Once the initial shyness about taking up the game has been overcome, any woman is going to be anxious to go out on the course and settle down to actual play. There are good reasons why her instructor won't allow this for a while. For one thing, it isn't fair to penalize other players, and that's exactly what it would be for a complete novice to sail back and forth down the fairway. Moreover, her ineptitude would probably send her straight back to the pro shop to turn in her clubs. It will be far better for the club members and for the golfer's own morale if she has absorbed the rudiments of the game during her lessons and worked out the worst kinks on the practice tee. Like learning to dance—or cook—golfing is not something that comes through osmosis, and I would warn any woman taking up the game not to be discouraged. However, most people, male and female, who want to learn golf are likely to be so strongly motivated that discouragement usually turns out to be a temporary thing. I feel that women, especially, must realize that becoming an able golfer takes time. It takes time, not because women are less adequate than men on the golf course, but simply because it is a process of learning and assimilation. So many women have engaged in sports so little since their school days —if indeed they were active then—that it requires training for unused muscles to become disciplined to the rigors of a golf game. But remember that fox trot.

Also remember women have a psychological advantage. A man is expected to pick up a club and break

13

90 before he's spent twenty hours on the course. A woman not only is not expected to be so adept, but usually she is considered a pretty helpless little thing, totally unable to introduce clubhead to ball. There are no added pressures in her learning process.

I'd like to say one final practical word about golf for women. Golf is really three games. There's the long game, where women are at a disadvantage. There's the short game, where women are at no disadvantage at all; in fact, if they've worked on their co-ordination and perception, they are ahead of that game by a mile. And then there is the game that is really eighteen games in one. Each hole is a miniature golf game, an individual challenge, an individual chance to "feel" the pitfalls of the course and attempt to beat the odds. Women are marvelous at this kind of thinking. A woman can and does think of a particular hole (say, a par five) as a small world in itself. As a matter of fact, this is where the "thinking game" comes in. Tommy Armour, one of the finest golfers and teaching pros of all time, knows this and has preached it for years. And before Tommy, there was Walter Hagen, perhaps the all-time great, who flatly refused to think about the hole he had just played or the one that was ahead of him. The only pin in the world for Hagen was the one he was shooting for at that minute. This is campaigning, and here the ladies are masters—or mistresses, if you insist. The only additional tip I can give is: Avoid self-pity at all costs. It will ruin a game faster than four bogies in quick succession!

So, it may take a year before a woman feels comfortable on the course. It will take longer before her handicap is as low as her husband's. It won't take even a year, however, before she begins to realize that while her golf game will be different from a man's, it can most certainly be just as good. What's even more important, it will be one that will give her all the self-confidence in the world, since she will come to appreciate her own deftness, sensitivity, and capacity for meeting a situation coolly. And she will learn to use her non-aggressive, but competitive, spirit. All a woman has to remember is that if she can walk, she can play golf!

Now, let's really get down to cases. In the following chapters, the finest pros in the business discuss an area of golf in which each is outstanding. No one can beat Marlene Hagge at pulling out of a seemingly impossible lie. Anyone who has ever watched Beverly Hanson hit the long irons cannot doubt her control or the power behind it. In a few particulars, these golfers will contradict each other. That's good—for golf and its players. Golf is a highly individual game. Barbara Romack, one of the really fine performers, tells us that she doesn't allow her hands to turn over in a punch shot; I do. My suggestion to the golfer is to try it both ways. The method that's most comfortable is the one that will produce results for you.

The next two pages will give you some idea of the way I teach the fundamentals of golf. From there on in, the chapters speak for themselves. Some of the points made by the pros are underscored by appearing in bold type and are brightly illustrated by mannequins designed to give you a rough idea of the principle involved.

Women may not have the muscle; they do have the intelligence. And also, I think, the sense of humor that golf demands. This last is a necessity, for golf is very much like a love affair: if you don't take it seriously, it's no fun; if you do, it breaks your heart. Don't break your heart, but flirt with the possibility.

The Fundamentals: Louise Suggs

*To start the grip, the club is laid across the
palm of the left hand, the club sole flush with the ground,
the top of the shaft pointing directly upward*

*As the left hand closes over the club shaft,
the "V" between the thumb and forefinger is in a straight
line with the player's right shoulder*

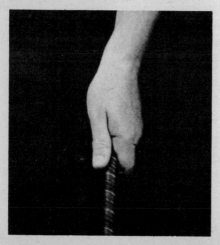

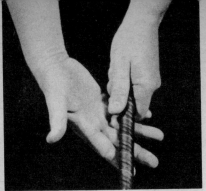

*The right hand is then laid on. In the basic
grip, the fingers are spread slightly, and the greatest
pressure applied by the first three fingers*

*As the right hand folds over into position, the
"V"'s of the hands are almost parallel. The right thumb,
uppermost when in place, is another pressure point*

*Looking at the grip from below, it may be seen
that the right pinky rests on the left forefinger, is the main
contact between the hands, keeps them working together*

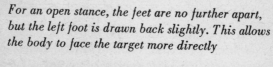

For a square stance, the feet are comfortably apart,
but never wider than the shoulders, and are parallel with
the target. The ball is centered between the feet

For a closed stance, the right foot is drawn back
from the line of flight, turning the body away from the
target. Otherwise the feet remain in position

For an open stance, the feet are no further apart,
but the left foot is drawn back slightly. This allows
the body to face the target more directly

At the top of the backswing, the wrists are
cocked, the left side has moved into the right, and
the head is still in position over the ball

At the end of the follow-through, the weight has
shifted left and in the transition, the right foot pivots,
allowing the head and body to follow the ball

The distance the player stands from the ball
is determined by the length of the club shaft. Here,
Louise Suggs demonstrates with an iron

Correct address demands that the arms hang
naturally while the sole of the club is flush with the
fairway. With a wood, the ball is further away

Chapter 2

The Short Irons
by Barbara Romack

These clubs are the secret of low scoring

• *Barbara Romack is the extremely attractive, extremely talented professional who walked away with the North and South title in 1952 at the age of 19, the Canadian Open championship in 1953, and the National Amateur title in 1954. She was a member and star of the U.S.A.'s last three Curtis Cup teams, the Florida East Coast champion in 1957 and 1958, and the Palm Beach champion in 1957. She plays her native California courses as though she owned them.*

In addition to her golfing interests, Miss Romack has been affiliated with The New York Life Insurance Co., is interested in fashion design, fascinated by public relations and is constantly on the go.

Barbara Romack believes strongly that women can play a better-than-average game of golf without turning into "golf nuts" — her own term. She is small (5'4", 109 pounds), but like another champion, Marlene Hagge, she is convinced that a woman does not have to be outsized to compete on the fairways. This chapter proves her point.

THE SHORT IRONS: BARBARA ROMACK

• Aside from the putter and wedge, the short irons are the most important clubs we gals have in our bags. Since they are used for short distances on into the pin (anywhere from 100 yards from the green), these are your birdie or scoring clubs — the clubs that will card your 90's, 85's, and 80's. And the secret of these clubs is that they are *made* for women.

When you use your short irons, forget about power. Strike the word from your golf vocabulary. The short irons can be used to their best advantage when the golfer thinks of each shot only in terms of accuracy. The correct grip and stance, a delicate but firm stroke, and your ball should be within a radius of 15 feet from the pin. When you can bring off your short iron shots so that this pleasant situation is consistent, you've got it made!

In using the seven, eight, and nine irons, almost all of the important action takes place through the hands and wrists. For years, women have felt inadequate about their golf game because they've felt that they haven't enough strength in their wrists and hands. Not so. Actually, women have a great deal of strength there, and in addition, they have a precision — almost a delicacy—that men don't have that will bring them out ahead.

FUNDAMENTALS

Let's get down to some of the basics in swinging these short irons. Remember first that swinging a short iron is a simple swing. It's what I call a one-piece swing, with the hands, arms, and clubhead all moving together, backed by a conscious control of your weight. This last factor brings in footwork and action through the legs — another area in which women are particularly limber and adroit, giving them another advantage.

In this swing I'm talking about, the movement is from shoulder to shoulder — a rocking motion of great fluidity. Not a push. Instead, you should feel as though your arm sockets were oiled. This encourages the authority that is so necessary in the three-quarter swing I'm discussing. Why three-quarter? Because your backswing is never quite as extended as it is with the mid- and long irons and, if your swing is executed properly, you don't wind up with the club wrapped around your neck. Always, you control the motion; it does not control you.

Item #1 for the fundamentals is alignment. This figures, since we're striving for accuracy and the alignment will largely determine where the ball goes. Use the sole of your club to line up toward the hole. Here, I'll pass on a tip that was given to me last year by another pro and that has helped my own game immeasurably. Keep the ball on a line with your nose. It's that simple. This means your ball is centered (which is true of most iron shots, by the way). The only time you change the position of the ball is for downhill or uphill lies — and we'll come to those. Now line your feet up a little on the open side, which means that your hips and shoulders will be looser too. Actually this alignment automatically restricts your swing to that three-quarter version I've mentioned before—and so emphatically.

There's very little body action involved, but the hands are lively as all get-out with short irons. This is because you simply can't guide the shot in even though we're reaching for precision. Instead, your hands are very strong on the club at all times. At the address, they are set slightly ahead of the ball, with the left

hand leading the shot from start to finish. The ball is hit with a descending blow, without any element of hurry. Never rush your swing and — most important — on every shot with your short irons, let both hands go out toward the hole.

One word here about the differences between the seven, eight and nine irons. In hitting the nine, a little more authority is called for, since the face is more open, but the seven and eight take longer swings.

HANDS AND WRISTS—PUNCH SHOTS

I've done a lot of talking about the hands and the importance of wrist action in using the short irons. One of my favorite shots is also one that will prove invaluable to your game. This is the punch-shot, for which I usually use a seven. At the same time, it is a shot that will strengthen those hands and wrists while you're practicing and increase your flexibility immeasurably. I use this on the course when I'm playing low and into the wind. To start, choke the club down from the end of your grip — about an inch and a half — and take only a half swing. I don't cock my wrists until my hands are past my right knee and from there, I cock them very abruptly. My hands are ahead of the clubhead, with the left hand leading from start to finish. The clubhead is square on this shot, on the closed side at the address, the ball back a little toward my right foot. My weight is more on the left side. The shot is hit a definite descending blow; remember you do not want the wind (either a real wind or one imagined for practice) to affect the flight of the ball. Remember too, if you are actually playing into the wind on a punch shot, you can't expect to get

24   the full distance from a short iron. You'll get about

85 or 90 yards when the shot is right. Most important: the hands do *not* turn over at all until the ball is on its way.

UPHILL LIES

The short irons also make your life easier for the downhill-uphill lies, and even the best of us find plenty of those. To begin with, in a situation where the feet are at a lower level than the ball, you must first counteract this by assuming a square stance and again, choking down on the club about an inch and a half. Since on most uphill lies, it's easy to whip or roll around on the shot because of the contour of the ground, I open the face of the club (say a seven) slightly to offset any small roll or hook, and in addition, I aim a little to the right of the pin. Now when I come down, I'm going to pull through strongly with my left hand — and both hands will very definitely be leading the clubhead. In going on through, I'll check my finish a little past waist-high or shoulder-high, whichever can be accomplished without losing my balance. Remember, the ball must get up and off.

DOWNHILL LIES

For downhill lies, your procedure is reversed at some points. In the average situation where the ball is below your feet, you must bend a little from the waist to get down to the shot, because if you don't you'll catch the ball square in the middle. Flex the knees slightly and assume a square stance, but this time a little on the open side, since the ball will probably have a tendency to slice somewhat. In order to further counterbalance this last factor, keep the clubface square, or opened according to the severity of the lie, but aim a little to the left of flag. Again, the hands are ahead of the club, with the left hand in the lead, but here, swing through to a good, full finish.

I find that if I take the clubhead a little on the outside of the line of flight, I can avoid hitting it into the hill on the way back. While coming down to the ball, the left hand is still in command, and the right side moves into the shot more quickly.

I think I should say something at this point about my qualifying adjectives. "A little more," "a bit more," "slightly longer" — these are all vague; but this is of necessity the only way to describe these situations in words. You will find that it's much easier to work out these same problems with a club in your hand rather than a book.

And while we're on *that* subject, it seems to me that before you begin to worry about your short irons, or your punch shot, or indeed the game of golf itself, you must decide what you're playing *for*. If you're going out to whack a ball around a course, then what I've been talking about isn't really terribly important. But if you want to play with your husband, or three other women who enjoy their game, then by all means don't be afraid to show your interest. You don't have to be a nut to get a lesson a week (at the very least, one every two weeks) and follow that up with one afternoon of solitary practice. Work some of those kinks out in private — just you, your head and your club. Finally, play twice a week if you can; once on Ladies' Day and on the weekend with your husband. If you practice those punch shots and ignore the disdain of certain masculine elements in the golf world, you'll soon find yourself in the happy position of being asked to play golf.

The Practice Tee:
Short Irons—Barbara Romack

In pictures and dialogue—an actual lesson

BARBARA ROMACK:
To warm up a bit, hit a few with the nine iron.
You don't have to be too precise to begin with.
What's your main difficulty with short irons?
PUPIL:
Most of the time I hit straight for the green, but recently,
I've been pushing to the right. If there's a sand trap there,
I always make it.
Okay, let's see you hit a few more balls so I'll
get an idea of how you swing.

Well, the first thing I notice is that you're taking too much swing. Think more of pulling your right shoulder away from your left shoulder. And I'd back away from the ball just a bit: You're too close.

Let's check your grip, Ruth. Now, assume your normal grip. Remember, you want to set this left hand so that you do not turn the club coming through. On these short shots you want accuracy, so you must go straight through.
From the inside out?
From the inside through, not out. Inside and straight through!

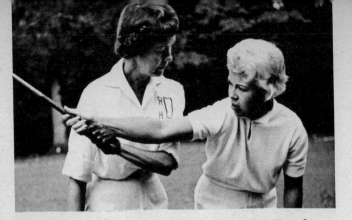

The club is taken straight back from the ball and swung in an arc up to the shoulder and then down on the inside. Try to aim at the back of the ball and hit down on its inside. We want to make this short and compact.

I'd line up first with the green?

Yes, you take the sole of your club and square it with your objective.

Okay, let's see how we shoot . . . Much better!

I hit the ball at the right spot, I suppose.

That's right. Did you realize how much loft you got? You were getting it up in the air with no apparent effort on your part. The loft of the club will always put it up there, if you don't try to help it.

Was the position of my feet correct?
Well, you could spread a little like this. Make
sure you get your weight a little more on your left
side and from the ball of the foot to the heel.
You have to dig the toes in on this a little, too.
Keep your hands a little more ahead of the club,
Your right hand on top. Do you have any
questions on this?

*If I want to make a short nine shot—in the air—to stop on
the green without rolling, how would I do that?*

**Shorten your grip on the club; choke it about half-
way down. Open the face of the club quite a bit—
like this. Keep your hands set way ahead, and
when you come down, really give it a whack with the
right hand as you come through.**

In other words, it would be more or less a half-swing?

31

Yes, that's right. On this shot, we open the face a little more. A little more wrist action to widen your hand action. You've been coming down too quickly. Stay down a little more. Let me demonstrate. My weight favors the left side. The arms and clubhead are all one—that's what you swing. And let the clubhead do the work. No pushing. When you get to here, break the wrists and let the clubhead come right on through the ball. It's really very simple. Keep your mind on that short grip; keep it halfway down the shaft, no matter how strange it may seem at first.

*Now—you try it again, Ruthie. Set your hands well
forward. That's better. But you're rolling your
hands over before you get to the ball. And your
left hand is a little weak. Be very firm in the
last three fingers of that hand. Not so tense . . .
just relax. Cock the wrists back of the right knee,
and that's as far as you want to go.*

*I'd like to get more distance out of the eight iron, Barbie.
You will. Remember that here too we're just swinging from shoulder to shoulder. Take a little longer
grip on the club. No, you're collapsing your left
arm, coming down. You're breaking it, and at that
halfway point, your elbow points out to the hole
like this before you get to the ball. We want to
keep it absolutely straight.*

Is my grip all right now?

**It looks much better. Put your right hand up on
top a little more and don't hold the club in; leave
it square. If you get that right hand too far under,
it makes you turn the club over. Set it more on
top so that you can swing it straighter back
in an arc.**

Should my shoulders be the same height?

**Your right shoulder will be a little bit lower be-
cause, actually, when you reach down and put your
right hand on the club, it does drop your shoulder
level a bit. Your shoulders are very good, but get
your weight on a more evenly distributed basis and
favor your left side—put more weight on it.**

Now, let me take a swing and you can copy it. Grip
your club down toward the middle. I'm doing this
for a reason—to liven up your hand action through
the ball so you don't try to guide and steer. I'm
going to take a very short backswing—to about
here. When I start down into it, I'll really try
to increase the hand action and get that right hand
zipping through so that we get a very decisive blow.
I'll break my wrists when the club is behind
my right knee.

That was a beauty!
The reason is that I saved all my decisive movement. I had no waste motion on my backswing. In
other words, I didn't take it way back and try to hit
from the back of my neck. I saved my push until
I got right down to the ball. You don't want to
use any strength taking the club back—or starting
your downswing until you get about waist-high.

Ruth, let's see you hit a few seven irons. The first thing to remember with the shorter irons is to set your hands more forward—well ahead of the ball. We do that so we can hit down on it. If you set your hands even with or behind the ball, then when you come into it, you're kind of scooping the ball. You won't have impact, firmness, or distance.

You hit that so the ball flew too low. Let's try to get it up in the air a bit. I want you to stay down; don't look up quite so quickly. And open up the clubface just a little. You tend to face the club on these short irons somewhat closed. Now, take a fuller swing than with the eight or nine.

You must take more swing here—like that. Just let the club get the ball up in the air; don't try to help it. When you get back and get set to come down, let the left hand lead and pop it! Let both hands in unison go out straight toward the hole!

So—Keep in Mind:

1. DON'T TRY TO POWER THE BALL — ACCURACY IS WHAT YOU'RE AFTER.

2. REMEMBER THAT THE HANDS, ARMS AND CLUB-HEAD ARE ONE UNIT IN YOUR SWING.

3. KEEP THE BALL ON A LINE WITH YOUR NOSE.

4. THE LEFT HAND LEADS FROM START TO FINISH.

5. ALWAYS LET BOTH HANDS GO OUT TOWARD THE HOLE.

6. FOR A PUNCH SHOT, CHOKE DOWN ON THE CLUB ABOUT AN INCH-AND-A-HALF.

7. DON'T COCK YOUR WRISTS UNTIL THEY ARE PAST THE RIGHT KNEE, PARTICULARLY ON THE PUNCH SHOT.

8. ON A DOWNHILL LIE, SWING THROUGH TO A FULL FINISH.

9. ON AN UPHILL LIE, THE FOLLOW-THROUGH MUST BE CONTAINED TO MAINTAIN BALANCE.

Chapter 3

The Medium Irons
by Ruth Jessen

The middle irons are the friendly indispensables

• *Ruth Jessen is a tall blonde with a formidable swing and a persistence in following through on detail that adds up to fine technique. She startled her home town of Seattle, Washington, in 1952 when she won the Women's City championship at the age of 16. Before she turned pro at 20, Miss Jessen improved her golf game to a point where she officially broke five course records, one of them with a 65 at the Redmond Golf Links, in Redmond, Washington.*

Since she became the youngest woman professional on the tour, this attractive golfer has won more than her share of purses, the climax being the Tampa Open title in 1959, although she had been plagued by disc trouble for that entire season. An ardent pianist with a secret yen to become a pop singer, Miss Jessen also likes to do a mean Charleston. Happily, however, she teaches — almost crusades for — her favorite sport, and for her favorite clubs, the middle irons. Here, she discusses these and explains why their proper use is essential to women.

THE MEDIUM IRONS: RUTH JESSEN

• The medium or middle irons — the four, five and six — are really the most valuable clubs in a woman golfer's bag. I make this statement for two reasons. First, they are the bridge between the short and the long irons. Second, the five is probably *the* club with which one should learn to play golf.

The five iron, a driver, and a putter were the clubs I had when I started, and needless to say they got quite a workout, particularly that reliable five. But through this workout, I learned just how important the midirons can be to one's game. Generally speaking, these clubs are the least complicated of any in the bag. At the same time, they are the ones that can do the most damage, or the most good.

With all irons, the number of the club indicates the loft of the clubface. The higher the number, the greater the loft. This gradation means that the player does not have to ease up on a club — or hit any harder — to arrive at the desired distance. This being so, the swing, the most important individual element in a player's game, can be established and maintained with little modification. This point is particularly important for women, who don't have the same power that men do, but who can obtain accuracy — and greater distance — simply by using a club with a lower number and less loft.

The stance — the way you place your feet and the distance between them — should measure approximately the width of your shoulders, and should be slightly open. Since the shafts of your irons are progressively shorter as the numbers increase, you'll find that you must bend over more on the midirons. But, as is the case with any club, never *lean* forward. Bend at the hips so that the sole of the club is flush with the fairway and make sure that you're comfortable in this position. Bending at the hips should also ensure the correct position for the head and eliminate the danger of bending *it* at still another angle. The ball is played midway between the feet on a five, slightly back toward the right foot for a six, and forward toward the left foot for the four. It seems that the main difficulty the beginner experiences with the irons is in not being able to hit the ball cleanly. She seems to feel that she must physically lift the ball with the club. Not true. In properly playing an iron shot for distance, you must hit down and through on the ball. The ball is not teed up; you must try to take a slight divot. It is a novice trick to try to get that little white orb into the air by pulling upward as the shot is hit. This only puts a smile on a dollar-and-a-quarter's investment!

Before going further, let's, for the sake of simplification, relegate the four iron to the category of long irons, which is where it really belongs. Since the four is designed for distance and control, the principles involved in dealing with the two and three will also apply to the four (see Chapter IV). We will concentrate on the five and six as the true midirons. The basic difference between these clubs is the distance that can be obtained from each and the bite or run the golfer can get from them. Now, the professional may expect to get 135 to 140 yards from a six, 150 yards from a five, and 155 to 165 yards from a four. Obviously, this can't be expected of a woman who doesn't play every day. For her, the rule of thumb is as follows: there is about a five- or ten-yard difference between any two consecutive irons. So whatever the average golfer gets with her two, she subtracts ten for the distance she can get with the three, and so on. This, of course, refers to the flight of the ball in the air. The amount of roll she'll get from the ball depends on the contour of the ground and the height from which the ball strikes the ground. The straighter the clubface, the more difficult it is to put backspin on the ball and thereby control the bite when it lands.

While the medium irons are the bridge between the distance clubs and the pitching clubs, the five virtually stands alone, since, in addition to spanning this gap, it is a club of multiple uses. The five is truly the "happy medium" of the golf bag. I've already said that it is *the* perfect club with which to learn. There are many reasons why this is so. For one thing, it is the club with which most women are truly comfortable, and for all golfers, but especially for a woman, confidence in a club and the distance and/or control she will get when she hits that club will be the difference between a good shot and lost par. Again, the five iron is a club with which, once they've grown accustomed to it, the ladies can get about 110-115 yards' distance. And since the five is generally the club that the beginner learns to handle first, it remains the best club in the bag with which to practice. By the time a woman has become a golfer, that five iron is an old friend. When the player picks it up, she automatically relaxes — a bonus not to be underestimated. It's the average club too, in the sense that it doesn't have too much loft or a face too straight. Having warmed up with the five, it's easier for the golfer to work either up or down the irons roster. For instance, it's obviously harder to time one's swing with a long-shafted club. The arc demanded by the two, three, or four is a wider, fuller one, and the player must warm up to it.

Starting with the five as the practice iron establishes more control.

Notice that women professionals use the five iron most often in demonstrating hooks, slices, high and low shots. It's a good club, say, for hitting into the wind. With the face slightly hooded, its loft allows a more nearly horizontal shot that keeps the ball true and gets the distance despite any fairway breeze.

One thing about the five and six that is sometimes overlooked is that they are fine clubs for approach shots as well as for distance. To take the six iron first, its face is not so deep as the seven iron, and the shaft is a little longer, so that it is good both for chipping *and* distance. The average woman player who hits her drive for around 150 yards can expect to get 90 or 100 from a six iron — which is not bad on the fairway. As for chipping, so much of the technique of approach shots depends on the contour of the ground and the position of the cup on the green that flat statements are hard to make. But, for example, if the cup is some distance from the edge of a fast green and the player is in a tight lie, the six would be the answer rather than one of the more lofted irons. Its straighter face would mean that, in this situation, the player would allow herself less margin for error. She'd get more run on her ball, which is what the shot calls for. Or, in another case, the six is excellent to use on a shot close to the green when the pin is near the green's edge and there's a slight hill between the ball and the hole. In a case such as this, it is best to use the six to hit into the bank so that the ball can hit and, hopefully, bounce over the hump to run toward the hole. Again, a short iron will bite too much for this type of lie. The ball will either hit the hill and roll back toward the player or just get over, bite, and then not run enough.

The five is also a handy little dandy for approach shots. Say there's a flat surface and the ball lies six or seven feet off the green. In this situation, rather than use an eight or nine iron and take the chance of stubbing or hitting behind the ball, which would only result in a flubbed shot, use the five. It will usually do the trick. Or the four or the six, depending on the distance you are from the pin. But in using the five, stand at a 45-degree angle to the hole and play the ball opposite your right foot. In playing a pitch-and-run shot with a medium iron, the ball is hit without a divot and the follow-through is the same as it would be for a putt. The clubface should be closed, or hooded, and it follows through toward the pin, which allows the ball to run with very little bite.

I can't emphasize strongly enough the importance of learning to hit these medium irons well. Golf, to repeat, is patterned on a basic swing; the medium irons allow the development of that swing. From there on in, the modifications are just that — modifications. The long irons and short ones take practice and more practice in order to become accustomed to their individual vagaries. This is true of the midirons as well, but their advantage lies in the fact that they pave the way for further development in the game. The very fact that you are working with clubs in which you have confidence will improve your mental attitude toward the entire game. Knowing one group of clubs intimately, it becomes easier to estimate the variations you'll need for the other groups. This is the strategic approach to golf, and since most women in no way resemble the muscular Hogans and Sneads, strategy is the only passport we have to excellence on the course.

The Practice Tee:
Medium Irons—Ruth Jessen

A pupil finds out more about the all-important five

RUTH JESSEN:
The first and most important thing in hitting the midirons, Pam, is your stance.
PUPIL:
Is this about it?
Well, it should be slightly open, which means drawing the left foot back a little, and the right foot slightly forward. This gives you more freedom of movement. Now, when you get into the short irons, you'll notice that many players exaggerate the spread. But for these medium irons, it is just slightly open.

Now, as you take this club away from the ball, it should go straight back through the line of flight. Notice that your wrists don't cock right away. But at about hip height, it begins to happen naturally. Notice, also, that as you come down into the ball, you hit against your left side, which means you are hitting down and through.

Is there any one thing I should watch out for, Ruth?
**Well, most beginners have one major fault: They're
always trying to scoop or lift the ball into the
air. I know I did when I started. Sometimes even
now, I press and do the same thing. You must hit
down through and take a divot. Pulling up
always means a weak shot.**

**One of the reasons that I consider the midirons so
important is that they build up to the other clubs.**
I thought you started with the woods?
**This is a mistake, Pam. If beginners would start
with these middle irons, they'd find the woods and
the other irons much easier. By using these clubs,
you will learn stance, backswing and follow-through
—the vital elements in using every club in the bag.**

47

Pam, one thing I notice is that instead of really bending at the hips, you're leaning toward the ball as you swing.

That's because I'm trying to keep my head down, Ruth.

But that won't help. Bend properly and your head will stay down. Notice that when you address the ball on your midirons, you don't lean or get to your toes. Firmness should be toward the left; a little more weight toward the left side.

*A slight bend in the knees makes your stance
relaxed. Stand as though you were lolling around;
the club is there because you're more comfortable
with it. It actually would be easier if the golfer
could just walk up to the ball, bend slightly, grasp
the club, put it down behind the ball and
swing through.*

Should my arms just hang at the address?
That's right. Just let your arms hang down in a
natural position, with your knees slightly bent so
that you're in a semi-sitting position, but not
squatting. Above all, you're comfortable.

*As you take the club away from the ball, the weight
goes to the right side. The weight shifts back as
you're hitting through the ball. This weight transition will be easier if you're in the position we
talked about—that is, bent slightly at the waist.*
*I see. Then I keep my head down because I'm bent over—
is that the idea?*
**That's it. But you never lean, because when a
player leans, she loses her balance.**

What was wrong with that last ball I hit, Ruth?
**You're lining the ball up to the hole with the top
part of your blade instead of the sole so that
you're really hooding the club. Now, set your club
and line it up with the base of the blade.**

*One thing I don't understand yet, Ruth, is when I'm on the
fairway, how do I know which iron to use?*

**This won't be much of an answer, Pam, but it's
really the only one I can give you. It takes time
before you gain that kind of judgment. How long
have you been playing now?**

About a year.

**Well, you'll find that the more you play, the more
you'll know when and how to use a club for a
specific distance. It's one of the most difficult
parts of the game at first, but once it becomes
more familiar, there won't be nearly so
much indecision.**

Let's go over to the putting green and I'll show
you a few approach shots with the five and six.
You know, many women will take the eight or nine
wedge or the seven iron for a short approach, but
they'd be better off with the medium irons. Let's
take the five, for instance. When I was telling
you about the open stance for the midirons before,
I meant it to be a lot less open than I'd like it
to be now. Here, you're just about facing the hole
with your body.

You mean I'm standing sideways?

Yes, in a way. The thing is, you're playing the
ball almost off the right foot. Your hands are
taking a real short grip on the club. The reason for
this is that most of the weight is on the left side.
And remember, when you take the club back, your
hands are ahead of the ball and they lead all the
way through the swing.

How about the backswing, Ruth?
I was just getting into that. When you take the
club away from the ball, it's a short stroke.
Actually, it's almost like a putt. It's a very precise
shot. If you hurry it, you skull or hit behind,
so watch that. You should be very deliberate.
On this shot, smoothness is very important. For a
short pitch shot, the arc is not as wide. Smooth-
ness becomes even more important since you have
less time in which to work in the swing.

53

Now, Pam, do you notice that you get more control this way? That's the whole reason for this stance. Your balance is better and everything works together. It's beginning to feel really comfortable. *I thought it would. Remember, a fairly short back-swing, the hands lead all the way through the shot and, above all, don't ever rush. Your stance is really open and you're bending—not leaning. You'll see—you'll get used to the midirons in a hurry!*

54

So—Keep in Mind:

1. YOUR STANCE SHOULD BE APPROXIMATELY THE WIDTH OF YOUR SHOULDERS AND SLIGHTLY OPEN.

2. YOU MUST BEND A LITTLE MORE WITH THE MID-IRONS THAN THE WOODS OR LONG IRONS, BUT NEVER *LEAN* TOWARD THE BALL.

3. YOUR MEDIUM IRONS CAN BE USED PROFITABLY ON APPROACH SHOTS.

4. IN PLAYING AN IRON SHOT FOR DISTANCE, YOU TAKE A DIVOT; IN USING IT ON AN APPROACH, YOU DO NOT.

5. PRACTICE WITH THE FIVE IRON WARMS THE PLAYER UP FOR EASY SWINGING WITH EVERY OTHER IRON IN THE BAG.

Chapter 4

The Long Irons
by Beverly Hanson

Control of these irons is your secret weapon

• *Beverly Hanson is coiled steel on the golf course. Off the course, she is a gracious and charming woman who has been a newspaper writer and editor and a rancher. Originally from Fargo, North Dakota, she now makes her home in Indio, California.*

Her record speaks for itself. Miss Hanson turned to golf seriously in 1945; in 1950, she took the Women's National Amateur championship in Atlanta. And eight years later, she topped all LPGA players with total earnings of $12,639.55 and took home the 1958 Vare Trophy as lagniappe. Among other honors, 1959 saw Beverly take the American Women's Open and the Links Invitational, again in Atlanta. Dynamically active in the LPGA, this is a golfer who is as articulate in her teaching as she is distinctive when she has a close, all-or-nothing shot coming up. Miss Hanson thrives on competition and anyone who has seen her play will vouch for her lightning speed. One girl who is not afraid of the long irons, this may be the reason she uses—and explains—them so well.

57

THE LONG IRONS: BEVERLY HANSON

• The long irons are my favorite clubs. This is an odd preference, because for most women they're the terrors of the golf bag. This simply shouldn't be. It is my feeling that the long irons are the victims of a lot of adverse publicity, coupled with the natural reluctance on the part of every player to concentrate on clubs that *do* require intensive practice. But—let's take an objective look at these clubs.

It seems to me that women dislike the long irons mainly because they're afraid of the straighter, smaller faces. This is understandable, but it's unfortunate that more teachers don't point out that the longs are lighter, whippier, and, once under control, infinitely more accurate than any other club in the bag — except perhaps the putter.

In approaching a lesson with the long irons, I first try to get the pupil to relax, to get and stay loose. I want her to have the same flexibility in the knees that she has in dancing. Only this kind of flexibility produces the freedom through the shoulders that leads to a smooth and easy swing. For if the natural male swagger makes for more ease in swinging a club, his extra strength and power also get him into more trouble on the course. His problem is learning to control his power; a woman has the easier task of learning to build up to power. When a man makes a mistake with a long iron, he's in trouble—as well as in the rough. When a woman makes a mistake, she may fall short of the target, but the chances are that the ball will be approximately where she wanted it to go.

The successful way to use the two, three, and four irons is based entirely on swing. Now, if women do have a disadvantage in golf it is that they move from their hips almost exclusively, while the golf swing is a one-two movement that works out of the shoulders. A perfect illustration is the hula hoop. If you put a hula hoop on a woman, she can learn to use it in a matter of moments, but a hula hoop on a man is a hula hoop lost. He has to learn a completely new movement. Well, the same thing is true of a woman swinging a golf club. The woman golfer must learn to let her arms and shoulders swing freely away from her body; she must learn to use that one motion to describe an arc. Remember, a golf swing is actually a negative way of creating power. The power is held in check on the backswing; it builds up on the downswing, it springs into action coming through the ball, and it diminishes on the follow-through. But the power itself is produced by the arc, which in turn is produced solely by the shoulders and arms. The natural swagger with which a man walks produces a golf swing; it helps him to learn the motion more quickly than most women. But that doesn't for a moment mean that a woman can't learn it, or become just as proficient at it as a man.

I also tell my pupils that the stance gets wider as the number of the club decreases. In other words, it's widest for the two iron, narrowest for the nine. It should never be wider than the shoulders, but since the stance is the foundation for the swing, the more expansive swing demanded by the long irons demands a wider stance.

Having adopted a fairly wide stance, the pupil is swinging the club like a dream. She's loose and easy, both knees are flexible, and her hands are gripping the club correctly. It's a fine start, but that doesn't guarantee that the ball is going to travel 140 or 150 yards to the green. The difference between an iron

used well and a horror on the fairway lies at the point of contact between the clubhead and the ball. We've already established that a long iron has a straighter face than any other club. Okay. But don't let it throw you. If you want the ball to go true, rest the club on the ground, let the shaft lean toward the body, and grip the club as it truly lies. The same rule that applies to the use of other clubs follows for the long irons as well: If you want the ball to go low or to the left, close the face slightly; if you want to slice, open the face. Unless you're in an unnatural lie, let the face alone do the job for which it was designed; I meant what I said when I emphasized the control it is possible to get from a long iron. Any one of these clubs will respond to a hairsbreadth change in opening or closing the face.

A point that comes up here is the grip — and I could start a separate crusade on that! So many golfers are concerned about placing their right pinky in the correct position over the left index finger that they inevitably wind up with a weak wrist — "the slicer's grip," we call it. The most important thing you can do is to concentrate on getting the index finger and thumb of the right hand into place. Then let the rest of the fingers fall into line. In doing this, the golfer should think of the club as a gun and the right index finger as the trigger finger. This is the strong player's position. I'll say categorically that golf can be played without ever using the pinky. The forefinger and the thumb are the most important elements of the grip, and you will never play well without having them set properly.

What determines the choice among the two, three, and four irons? Well, several factors. Yardage, of course, is one of them. How long is the shot? And what distance do you get from each iron? What kind of green are you shooting at? Is it elevated or trapped, so that the ball must be lofted, or is the approach flat enough to permit the ball to roll or bounce to the green? If the green is soft and slow, your ball may carry onto it without skittering over the back edge and into trouble. If hard and fast, you may have to hit short and run up. Sometimes, when a golfer runs into a really hard green, she'll find herself playing what we call basketball golf. She'll have to dribble the ball up onto the green. In that case, if she's confronted with a shot of 150 yards, she certainly wouldn't take a two iron and strike for the pin. She'd take a three or four, let the ball hit short and bounce. Each circumstance finds its own solution and its own club. This is one of the most rewarding and most infuriating parts of golf: The player must eventually get to the point where her judgment in the choice of a club is as accurate as her swing.

At about this point, pupils usually ask: How often should I practice? How important is it? This depends on what the individual wants out of the game. Most people who are fond of golf go way beyond thinking of it as a hobby-sport. It assumes much more importance than the three or four hours it takes to go around a course. For them, I'd say that a couple of practice sessions a week are almost mandatory. There's another factor, too. If a woman's game has been going along smoothly, a lay-off of six days can produce something that I think of as an emotional shock when she picks up her clubs again. She'll be rusty for the first few holes at least and this can throw the rest of her game, as well as show up on the score card in a disconcerting way. If two practice sessions a week are difficult to manage, there's another answer. Try picking up a club and swinging it instead of sitting down with a magazine. Practice swinging in the back yard (or an uncluttered room, for that matter) as a filler while waiting for the groceries to be delivered — or during a coffee break — or instead of a short walk. Practice helps keep the shoulder muscles loose and, as with every other sport, the more familiar the equipment feels, the more adept the player will be in actual performance.

This sureness with the clubs is particularly important for a woman. Unsure of herself in this game to begin with, she is particularly susceptible to the well-meaning friend who comes along and destroys her confidence (and often her incentive) by saying, "Your stance is all off. And your grip could be improved. Why not try . . ." It's easy enough to become discouraged while the learning process is going on without family or friends suddenly appearing in the guise of unlicensed pros. When it happens, the golfer must ignore it and concentrate on the pointers she's picked up from her teacher and on those she's worked out for herself — and believe me, there'll be plenty of both.

Something I've found of immeasurable help to a woman is a series of simple hand-strengthening exercises. No woman needs an armful of bulging muscles to play golf, but strong forearms and wrists can make or break a golf game. Twisting a towel — wringing it — is one of the best exercises I know for just this purpose. I'm sure our grandmothers had much stronger wrists than we do. Washing machines hadn't made their appearance then. So our answer is this towel-wringing routine. One thing: the towel should be wrung inward, toward the body, rather than away, as ordinarily it would be. Squeezing a rubber ball is a good exercise, too. I'm not for a moment implying that one must become an addict to do this. Again, it's a question of those occasions, no matter how few, when fifteen minutes, thirty minutes, or an hour of exercise would not be a chore. Believe me, the results will be noticed on the course!

To sum up: I would unqualifiedly recommend to women seriously interested in their game that they devote more time to their long irons—and less apprehension. The irons will take care of a golfer in situations where the woods simply don't measure up. I've watched women practicing who usually call it a day when they get to the long irons. In a way, of course, they're smart to spend more time on the short irons, because that's where girls lower their score most quickly. But in ignoring the two, three, and four irons, they're missing a thrill; seeing a well-stroked ball go right to the pin is something of an achievement. Each club is worth so many yards, depending on the player's capability, and while there are instances where the five wood will do very nicely, with less trouble, there are others where an iron is the saving grace for par. Just don't be discouraged. The finest golfers don't always hit the long irons well, but if a certain proficiency can be attained with these most difficult clubs, there's no part of the game beyond attainment for the conscientious player. And once that happy situation is reached, a woman has beaten a game at which she is supposed to be inept. The supposition is wrong, and so are the people who make it. Golf is for everybody; "everybody" includes women—as golf includes the invaluable long irons.

The Practice Tee:
Long Irons — Beverly Hanson

A golfer wonders why she was afraid of the long irons

BEVERLY HANSON:
*Remember that the long irons are designed so that
you can take a longer backswing. Take advantage of
that to get a fuller, wider arc. That means you
can get more club speed and the faster you can bring
the clubhead through the ball, the farther the ball
is going to go.*
PUPIL:
*I try so hard to get the distance that I'm overpowering these
long irons and that's the wrong way to go about it.*
**That's all right, Martha, like everything else, it
means more practice. And of course, remember at
the same time that these are the irons you can get
accuracy with—you've got to think of that, too. A
wider, smoother arc—that's the way.**

I'm afraid I've got a mental block on the irons.
**That's natural, unfortunately! You've got plenty of
company. Now, let's take the address position.**
Does the face look open enough?
**That's fine. Always remember—the easiest changes
you can make in a golf swing are the changes you
make before you start swinging.**

In other words, changes you try making during the swing are almost always doomed since the entire swing takes only a couple of seconds, so your chances of correcting an error are better made while you're in address position. The errors that we make in that position account for 85 to 90 per cent of all mistakes made during the swing, anyway.

You'll find that the more you can work toward having an equal amount of knee flex at the address, the easier it will be to keep the right from stiffening on the backswing.

I'm so conscious of that right leg now—and that right knee.

Well, take the club and pretend you're dancing for a second. Just feel the mobility you'd have in your knees. Now take the club, throw it out in front of you with the same amount of bounce in your knees and feel how much more club speed you can get that way. Now you've got a swinging action.

That's wonderful position at the top! Do you feel now that you're swinging through to the finish?

But it's like a nine iron shot. How long will it take me to get distance?

Distance is a matter of being in position and trusting. You are just beginning to get position. You're going to have to hit quite a few to learn to get stronger release through the hitting area. The longer you can delay your clubhead release, the more distance you'll get. In other words, the only reason you swing a club back is to give yourself time to build speed on the way back down. Now, if you do go to the effort of making a good backswing and then you start releasing that power just as you start down, your club speed is going to be virtually nil when you reach the ball.

Another thing you might check on is your right-hand grip. I notice you tend to have that thumb way up and you're almost making a fist out of that hand. Spread it more. Let the index finger come farther down the shaft. You know the feeling that the index finger is the trigger finger? Well, that's what we want in golf. Remember that the thumb and forefinger help you determine when you release your blow. If you have that right hand balled up like a fist you have absolutely no way of conserving your club speed—of building up speed.

You want your wrists to begin to break—to relax— as you start your forward swing, and that trigger position will help you do this. Get as much of your right hand on the shaft as you can. Now grip it tightly. Make sure that the web between the thumb and forefinger is very closely knit together. Good. Let's go to the four iron now.

Do I have the same grip, Bev?

Actually, your grip is the same for all the clubs— with the exception of the putter.

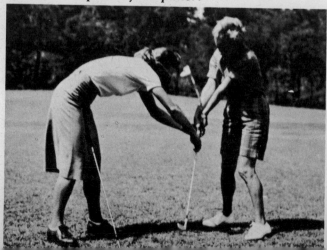

*Now you've got that right hand too much on top of
the left. Get as much of the right hand on
the club as you possibly can. When you have it
sitting on top of the left hand, you're playing
the game with only one hand.*

*I always thought my little finger on the right hand had to be
interlocked with the left hand.*

You mean actually interlocked?

No, I mean holding the left, I guess.

*Your right pinky can sit right on the knuckle of
the left index just as long as the two hands
work as a unit.*

*Do you feel that you're getting better
power with more right hand?*

I feel that I've got a lot more control, that's for sure.

*You'll find it will make 100 per cent difference
in your swing—in timing your release
and wrist action.*

If you're going to be a good player, it's a basic
rule of the game that the clubhead cannot pass the
hands until you have contacted the ball. At impact,
the clubhead and the hands should be no more
than parallel. If you're not using the right-
hand thumb and forefinger the way you should,
your swing breaks down. The clubhead passes the
hands before you've contacted the ball. Also, you
learn to sense where that clubhead is through
the use of thumb and forefinger of the right hand.
Get that trigger finger out there so that
the inside of the index finger is pushing right
against the side of the shaft.

I don't close the face of this club any more than I do?

No, Ma'am! Never close the club face unless
you want to hit low or to the left.

Supposing I'm in trees?

Then only if you want a low ball. Just leave the
club face alone. You're catching on to that knee
position quite well. Like a duck to water.

Does it feel pretty good?

It's beginning to be a lot more comfortable.

Fine. Now that we've got your confidence up,
let's move on to the two iron—that's the wicked one.

Just what is the difference, Bev? Does it change my grip, or stance, or swing?

The difference is practically nil. The grip and the stance are the same. You can anticipate a little longer shot—again because of a slightly longer shaft. And you can expect a slightly lower ball because of a straighter club face.

More than a three?

Only a fraction more. The two iron seems to be everybody's candidate for an unfavorite club because it is the most difficult iron to handle. Many players are going to the five wood because it's so easy, but I personally think the two iron merits attention. Your swing is essentially the same; just because there's a #2 on the bottom of the club shouldn't throw a golfer into a tailspin.

Do you think I should get as much distance with my two iron as with my five wood?

Definitely.

But not loft.

In time, you'll get almost the same loft as well.

I felt that index finger. It makes a tremendous difference.

Doesn't it? You know just where the club is. You have excellent right elbow position, too, Martha —at the top of your backswing, your right elbow is pointed toward the ground and that's something I like to see in a golfer. If that elbow is tossed off into the air, it's too easy for the right side to take complete charge at the start of the downswing and you'll find yourself going outside of the ball and chopping down.

71

*I find it's very hard to concentrate on two things while
hitting the ball; I either have to think of one or the other.*

**That's a good point, Martha. Actually, I think
that every golfer who's still learning the game
is wisest if she takes one point and sticks to it
until it becomes part of her game. If you leap-
frog from point to point, you confuse a difficult
game even more. There's nothing in one's back-
ground to prepare for a golf swing. For that
reason, it's sounder to take one point and
stick to it before moving on to the next.**

Until it's natural.

**Until it's a part of you and your swing. Then
you'll find that when you approach the ball, there's
one more detail you can forget about.**

I wish my swing would straighten out.

**Well, that fault is the result of a slight break-
down of the right wrist as you're coming to the ball.
That opens the club face which sends the ball off
to the right. But the more familiar you become
with the grip, the easier it will be for you
to drive straight on through. If you're going to hit
the ball straight, the club face must be square
when it contacts the ball.**

*You mean I should bring it back through the way you've just
done—as though I were leading the ball?*

**Well, you'll learn to sense the position of the
clubhead as you become more familiar with
the trigger-like grip.**

That's much better, Martha. You don't look as though you're quite as afraid of these long irons as you were.

I love them now. I never understood them before and I'd never use them, but you're right—I'm not afraid now.

Good! Really, this game isn't as complicated as people have made it. You only have one swing, and you use it all the way through. The only changes that take place are the increasing wideness of your stance as the clubs get lower in number—so your arcs will get wider and your swing a little fuller. But too many people think you have a completely different swing with a six iron than you would have with a two or three and it isn't true. One swing carries through.

I'm glad to be reassured that the swing holds for all clubs. I had worried about the differences among the clubs.

Well, as I've mentioned, we have a slightly wider stance as the clubs get longer simply because the swing gets bigger and we need a bigger base on which to operate. Just keep using your fundamental swing whether you're working with a three or an eight. Remember that you can describe a wider arc because the shaft of these long irons is longer.

My grip still doesn't seem quite right.

I'll tell you one thing that might help you, Martha. When many golfers put their right hand on the club—they're so concerned about the little finger and getting it into position that it's the first part of the right hand that they put on the club. In doing this, they put themselves in the slicer's position. Now, instead of worrying about that little finger, get that trigger finger and the thumb on first. The last thing to put on is the little finger.

That makes it easier. I was too conscious of that little finger.
**Very good. Now, you notice people who are obviously
beginners. They'll walk up to the ball and then
seem almost to count as they put each finger on
the club to make sure they've got all ten of
them. Invariably, in putting that right hand on,
they come under the club to get that pinky on
and they're already set in the slicer's position.
They don't have to do anything else to make
sure they go off to the right.**

**But your strong player
will put his hand on like this ...**
He puts his thumb and index finger on first.
**That's right—because that's the important part
of the grip. You can play golf very successfully
and never even have your little finger on the club.
You can just leave it off. But I promise you this—
you will never play golf well without having the
thumb and forefinger of your right hand on
the club properly!**

So—Keep in Mind:

1. AS THE CLUB GETS LONGER, THE STANCE GETS WIDER.

2. IN ESTABLISHING YOUR GRIP, THINK OF THE CLUB AS A GUN AND YOUR RIGHT FOREFINGER AS THE TRIGGER FINGER. SETTING THIS FINGER AND THE RIGHT THUMB ON THE CLUB IS THE MOST IMPORTANT PART OF THE GRIP.

3. THE ARC OF THE SWING IS PRODUCED BY MOVING THE SHOULDERS AS ONE UNIT.

4. DEVELOP FLEXIBILITY IN BOTH KNEES.

5. UNLESS YOU ARE SHOOTING FROM SLOPING GROUND, KEEP THE CLUBFACE SQUARE, OR TRUE.

6. PRACTICE TWICE A WEEK IS ESSENTIAL.

7. SIMPLE HAND-AND-WRIST EXERCISES WILL STRENGTHEN YOUR WRISTS AND FOREARMS FOR POWER.

8. PRACTICE FAITHFULLY EVERYTHING YOUR PRO TELLS YOU.

Chapter 5

The Fairway Woods by Joyce Ziske

When you pick up a wood, you pick up distance

• *Joyce Ziske is a friendly, quiet girl whose natural athletic ability has made her a standout on golf courses across the country. Environment probably had something to do with the development of her fine golf game — the Ziske home in Wisconsin was adjacent to a driving range. As with many other professionals, once the youngster had discovered the challenge latent in a set of clubs, the woman was determined to show what she could do with them.*

At 15, Miss Ziske won the Wisconsin Junior Consolation and was on her way. By 1954, she had come up with her second Wisconsin State Women's championship and victories in the Palm Beach and North-and-South Amateurs, but these took second place to the honor that had been a dream for years: Joyce Ziske was on the 1954 Curtis Cup Team. She was also on her way as a pro.

An enthusiast of French poodles, horses, and music, Joyce Ziske is vocal on one point. "Of course women can play golf! We're people, too, aren't we?"

THE FAIRWAY WOODS: JOYCE ZISKE

• I'm the best example I know of a golfer to whom the fairway woods are indispensable. I use them because I need the distance. No one can play tournament golf without hitting the long shots into the green well, and the woods are designed for power and distance. For the average woman player, the problem is not that of a tournament player, but getting distance is still important. Since a great many women do not like the long irons (or are afraid of them), the woods, with their larger faces and longer shafts, are the answer. If a player can learn to handle these adroitly, she'll have the distance that, along with a solid short game, will make her a fine player. In addition, these clubs have specific purposes that the irons just can't fill.

Because the three, four, and five woods are more lofted than the corresponding irons, and because they have longer shafts, they'll hit higher and farther, and the allowable margin of error is a little greater as well. I don't mean that any golfer should ever think in terms of a margin of error, but most players feel more confident knowing that a cushion is there. Now, since these woods for the most part will go farther than your long irons, it means that women can make the par threes and fours—and even the fives—when they can't possibly cover the distance in par with their long irons.

By this I don't mean to imply that anyone can pick up a wood and hit the green every time. Like putting or driving, the fairway has its own rules and demands, if the player is to execute the shot successfully. One of these rules is that she must be able to choose her wood correctly for a given situation. For instance, the four wood will get the ball up in the air with a little less loft than a five, but it will always sail more with the wind, which makes it the preferred club to use over traps. The three wood will hit an even lower shot than a four and is a good bet when you're forced to play into the wind. As for the two, most women aren't strong enough to use this club very successfully. Those few women who are, usually use it off the tee. On a fairway, if you have a lie that's good enough for a two wood, you can use your driver.

This seems a pretty abrupt summation of the differences among these clubs, but it would require a book in itself to cover all of the contingencies that can arise. Only by playing the game over a period of time can anyone sharpen her judgment to a point where the choice of club is almost automatic. Even professionals, playing the same course day after day, find themselves in situations where they must hesitate before calling for a club, which only means that golf is no game for a robot. This is one of its more attractive features, however, for no other game offers so much mental and physical stimulation.

I can't emphasize strongly enough the importance of learning to use the woods properly. Unless a woman has become really adept at playing her woods, she has lost the game before she starts. After all, we're talking now about woods versus long irons, and if the woods are not used expertly, the player is in just as bad a spot as she would be if she were unable or unwilling to play the long irons.

Another factor here is the amount of time women give to practice. By and large, a woman will not practice as long or hard as a man. There are many reasons for this. One of them is that her leisure time is more broken up—by PTA meetings, Scout meetings, church groups—all the diversions the community has created

for feminine service and recreation. Whatever the reason, it is unlikely that her attention will be as intensive or as regular as a man's when it comes to focusing on just one group of golf clubs, and it is undeniably true that the long irons require concentrated work.

It may not be out of place here to go over that basic element, the grip, since, along with the swing, it is the foundation of the game. In using the fairway woods, the club is placed diagonally across the palm of the left hand. The hand is then closed over the shaft, so that the "V" between the forefinger and thumb is aimed at the right shoulder. The webbing between these two digits should be extremely close. The right hand's pinky closes over the left hand's index finger. This is the grip used for all golf shots, but I'm emphasizing it here for the sake of underlining this detail: never, I repeat, never let that "V" open up or spread. This will cause a lot of trouble with any clubs, but particularly with the woods.

Tight webbing ensures a firm grip and an authoritative stroke. Authority is something to be desired in any phase of the game, but it is mandatory when it comes to something as decisive as a shot involving 140 or 150 yards. The stance should be slightly open; comfortably open, so that your balance is at the optimum. The ball, for all of the woods, is played off the left heel.

Whether we're discussing the long game or the short game, the decisive element must be the swing. For the woods especially, the swing is the focal point of good performance. And swinging with the woods is really easier for the woman than it is for the man, because it's absolutely necessary that the swing not be a lunge, or even a fiercely powered whack. It's a sweeping, dusting motion — all one movement, designed to get the ball up and off. The player should always sweep the ball, easily and firmly, but with enormous authority. It might help to remember that one of the reasons she's using a wood is because of the extra loft it offers. If she lets that loft do the work for her, she can stop fretting about either height or distance because she'll get both. Her only concern should be in staying relaxed and hitting into a firm left side to maintain the rhythm of the swing. The ball will fly truly if she hits truly, within herself. I don't mean that there is no exertion in connection with a wood. Of course there is. But the exertion comes from the build-up inherent in a good swing, not in an attempt to slam the ball two holes beyond the pin she's aiming at.

UPHILL LIES

From an uphill lie, where there is a fairly steep grade, the ball is played forward, so that when the player swings, the bottom of the arc will be toward the left foot. In addition to the hazard these uphill lies offer in themselves, the golfer will have a tendency to hook the ball, so she must aim to the right for it to draw in toward the hole.

DOWNHILL LIES

On a downhill lie, the bottom of the arc is toward the player's right foot, so she should place the ball toward that foot. In that way, she will be swinging with the slope of the hill, and can get to the ball before she contacts the turf. If she plays a downhill lie as she does a regular shot on the flat, nine times out of ten she will catch turf and fan the ball. And, on these lies, there will be a tendency to slice. To offset it, the player should face slightly left of the green.

For these downhill lies, it's also important that the player remain relaxed throughout the entire body. If she pulls up and away because of tension through the legs and torso, she'll catch the top of the ball—if she doesn't fan it completely—and perhaps make the lie even worse. After all, the body should, at least, stay on the same level with the ball.

On these unnatural lies, too, there is likely to be the added hazard of *having* to slice or hook to bring the shot home. Here, cold comfort though it may be, the amateur is on a level with the pro, since even the latter, while she's played a lot more golf, must think very consciously of the amendments to the ordinary shot demanded by a deliberate hit either to the right or left. For a hook she should lift her left hand toward the top of the club and drop the right toward her right side. For a slice, she does just the opposite; everything moves toward the left. The player must also change her stance. For a slice, the stance is opened, the right foot drawn closer to the ball, the left foot away from it. On a hook, she moves the left foot toward the ball and the right foot away. The only advice any pro can give a golfer under these circumstances is to try to stay calm.

"Stay calm" might well be the motto for the entire game, and most particularly for women. I think that women's only disadvantage in playing golf is that they're afraid—afraid of seeming to dominate in an area usually reserved for men, afraid maybe of beating the men, and afraid that they'll make fools of themselves for trying! Especially does this fear seem to crop up when it comes to the long shots. If a woman is afraid she can't hit, she won't hit; if she's afraid she's going to slice, she'll slice. Above all, I'd recommend that if a player is afraid of hitting a particular shot, it is time to go out and practice the shot, because that's the one that will ruin her score, no matter how proficient she is in the rest of her game. As far as the fairway woods are concerned, I have always told my pupils that this is one area where they can cut at least a stroke from their game. If a golfer hits a halfway decent tee shot and then hits one of her woods, rather than a long iron she's unsure of, that extra confidence alone is going to mean she'll come in with a five instead of a six for that hole.

If I were asked to pinpoint the differences between the problems of men and women in playing golf, there's really only one I'd consider important. Men use brute strength, which hurts them; women don't hit strongly enough—which hurts them. They try to cue the ball. They're afraid to swing at it firmly. But both sexes still will get the club up to the top and try hitting it so hard from there, that by the time they get to the ball, there's nothing left. As a result, they lose their balance and their position. Lunging at the ball, muscling it—these won't work. A relaxed, steady, rhythmic swing is the only thing that will get the clubhead through the ball with proper speed for distance and accuracy.

If women will take advantage of their natural sense of rhythm and inject it into their swing, that rhythm, along with the confidence a fairway wood gives them, will take the fear out of golf. And once the fear is gone, any woman can play her husband a match for the grocery money and be pretty sure of a new hat!

The Practice Tee:
Fairway Woods—Joyce Ziske

Swinging for distance is really sweeping the woods

JOYCE ZISKE:

With your three wood begin the grip with your left hand. Lay the club across the palm diagonally. Make sure the webbing of the "V" between thumb and forefinger is close. This makes all the difference in the world in the strength of your grip.

PUPIL:

Sometimes I pop the ball straight up in the air— that really hurts!

Don't hit down on the ball ever. Just sweep it off the grass as you would a driver. The ball is played off the left heel as you would play any other wood shot—and sweep it up a bit and off. But never hit down on it.

*Very good! That was a fine hit! Now, Mary, stand
a little closer to the ball. When you're backed
away from it, you can't turn, so you can't relax.
When you move in, even a little bit, your body is
able to move into the ball. This is extremely
important.*

*You see, you stand a trifle closer and it will
make a difference. Let your arms just hang down
from your body. When you're out from the ball, your
whole torso automatically assumes a forced position.
You have a tendency to tighten up that left
side and you're too tense. Relax. Just swing
the club. and don't worry about anything else.*

*And—never hurry your swing. Make sure you have a
steady, smooth tempo all the way through. One
of the biggest mistakes a golfer can make is to
rush her swing. You may find that the left side
does straighten up, or that you grip too near the
top. Or that you overswing—but your main concern
should be to stay steady and smooth through that arc.*
I've heard a lot about getting up to the top and then just
letting fly.
**Forget most of what you've heard, Mary. The secret
of the woods is up and down in steady rhythm.**

*That's good, very good! Your swing was rushed a
little, even though it was a fine hit. Remember,
Mary, when you rush, you're going to get way ahead
of the ball. As a result, you'll straighten up,
and then you're going to hit behind the ball
because your shoulder drops.*

I've always been teased about overswinging.

*You don't overswing—the only time a golfer over-
swings is when he or she loses sight of the ball at
the top of the swing—and you don't.*

Now, let's take the four wood. That's also played
off the left heel—a little in back of it as we
did the three. That part of it is about the same.
This club has a lot of loft to it. It will get the
ball into the air faster—and it carries a trifle
short of the three wood. Again, the loft will get
it into the air for you; don't try to help it.
And you swing this club just as you would any
other fairway wood.

I hit down on that last one, didn't I?

That's right. You tried extra hard, and when you
do that, you break the rhythm of the swing. Also,
be sure you don't get that right hand on top again,
Mary. Keep it down so the "V" is pointing at
your shoulder.

That's very good. You couldn't hit one much better.
If it would just stay with me!
**It will! You only have to believe it's going to.
There are a few things you have to watch and one of
them is getting that right hand over on top.
Another thing, don't tighten up when you're coming
into the ball. That's why you sometimes drop down
into it . . . and hit to hazards.**

Now that one you hit very wide.
What's that from? Trying too hard?
**Well, you weren't set to start with. When you're
set, keep your weight on the inside of your feet,
then stop thinking about it. So many people
worry about where the weight should be that it
interferes with their swing. If you relax, that
will take care of the problem.**

That was fine. You only have to concentrate on relaxation and you'll be all right.

But didn't I come in a little late on that one?

Well, it changed the tempo of your swing. I know I sound like a broken record, but golf really is a matter of relaxing. Everybody thinks it's much more. It's merely a question of finding rhythm and balance.

And that's the hardest thing in the world to get! I don't know many people who can relax with their golf.

It gets under your skin.

Well, if you let it, your game will never be what you want it to. Let's hit one more since you pulled that one and then go to the five.

Fine!

Do you use your five wood out of the rough? I use it for practically everything.

Well, the five can be used out of roughs; it can even be used out of traps on rare occasions; it can be used out of divots—it's just about the handiest club in the bag. To use it effectively is just a matter of practice and confidence.

One of the reasons it's so good for the rough is its small head. That means it will cut right through the grass, where the irons will go into the grass and you have to be very strong to pull them out. Now, play the ball between center and your left heel. Actually, in golf all the clubs are played from the same place—that left heel. Most players make the mistake of thinking that they're played farther back. Here you play it off your left heel, but you change your stance.

Now I said that it's always off the heel of that left foot. The woods are played right there. It only looks different because you must move your stance. Whether I'm using a wedge, fairway wood, nine iron, driver, that heel is the point of reference every time, because you do use the same pattern and the same swing. There's only one low point in your swing and that's where the ball is. That's why I never change the basics. If you place the ball at the low point of your swing, it automatically relates to that heel. And you move accordingly—a little closer for your nine iron, back for the fairway wood, but the focus remains the same.

As soon as you don't relax and swing the club easily,
you'll pull up from the ball. You'll tighten up
and drop your shoulder and then you're certain to
hit behind it. Just swing the club easily. I can't
emphasize strongly enough how important this is.
Another point: with the five, you won't have to work
as hard. Let the loft do it. As soon as you work too
hard at it, you're going to miss it. Just swing
the club, take it back and through. 93

What about my stance? How wide should that be?
For the woods, a fairly wide stance is in order.
It should pretty well be determined by comfort,
since the more comfortable you are, the looser you'll
be. There's one major fault to watch for. A great
many people swing with the stance wider than their
shoulders and justify it by saying that they're
more comfortable that way. Don't. If the stance
is wider than the shoulders, you lose your balance.

So—Keep in Mind:

1. BECAUSE THE WOODS ARE MORE LOFTED THAN THE LONG IRONS, THEY'LL HIT HIGHER; BECAUSE OF LONGER SHAFTS, THEY'LL HIT FARTHER.

2. IF YOU HAVE A LIE THAT'S GOOD ENOUGH FOR A TWO WOOD, YOU CAN USE YOUR DRIVER.

3. IN CONSIDERING THE GRIP, REMEMBER TO KEEP THE "V" BETWEEN THE THUMB AND FOREFINGER TIGHT. TO LET IT SPREAD MEANS A RESULTING LOSS OF AUTHORITY.

4. THE BALL, FOR ALL OF THE WOODS, IS PLAYED OFF THE LEFT HEEL.

5. YOUR SWING SHOULD BE A FIRM SWEEPING MOTION, DESIGNED TO GET THE BALL UP AND OFF. *NEVER CHOP DOWN.*

6. TO HOOK, TURN THE LEFT HAND OVER THE TOP OF THE CLUB; DROP THE RIGHT HAND TOWARD THE RIGHT SIDE.

7. FOR A SLICE, THE PROCEDURE IS SIMPLY REVERSED; EVERYTHING MOVES TO THE LEFT.

8. REMEMBER THAT FEAR LOSES MORE STROKES THAN ANY OTHER FACTOR.

Chapter 6

The Drive
by Jackie Pung

This shot sets you up for the whole round

• *Hawaii doesn't mean pineapples and Waikiki to golf fans; it means Jackie Pung. Since 1953, when Mrs. Pung turned pro, she has demonstrated on and off the course that she is an invaluable contributor to a game that requires persistence and devotion.*

Popular with the sportswriters because of her cheerful volubility, Jackie Pung proved beyond any doubt that she was a champion when, having won the 1957 U.S. Women's Open, she unknowingly signed a card that had been incorrectly scored by her partner, and so was disqualified. The picture carried in the newspapers the next day showed the partner in tears, being comforted by Mrs. P. A stern competitor, she has won the Northern California Open, the U.S. Women's Amateur, the Triangle Round Robin, and the Sea Island and Jacksonville Opens, among others. In her off-tour time, she is a homemaker par excellence, a devoted mother and a teaching professional. A long hitter, Mrs. Pung believes the drive is an easy shot. She makes it seem so in the following pages.

THE DRIVE: JACKIE PUNG

For the drive, those basic elements of any golf swing—the grip, stance, body position, and rhythm—remain the most important, after all.

First, the player must realize that she is now dealing with a long-shafted club and that, in order to keep the left arm straight, it will be necessary to develop a little extra strength in that hand and side. This is achieved by keeping the hands even with, or slightly forward of, the ball at address.

The trap that we women most commonly fall into is that of taking the club back with the right hand and then letting the right elbow fly—really meaning to point or bend outward—**rather than keeping it tucked close to the body.** This error is then made even worse by turning the swing into a downward chop. All of this can be taken care of, however, if that left hand and arm are strengthened to the point where they are in control all the way through the shot.

The golfer's footwork also contributes to control. The knees must remain flexible and the weight forward a bit—on the insteps. If the player stands flat-footed, she won't be able to make the weight shift necessary for the pivot.

Now, along with firmness through the left side, flexibility must be maintained as well. This permits the shoulders to be rotated during the swing, while the body itself acts as a center pole or axis, and the head and eyes remain glued on the spot where the ball lies. Here is another extremely important point: the head must *not* bob up. If it does, the smooth swing will be spoiled. The shoulder will move up as the club is brought back, and the arc of the club on the downward swing just won't sweep through the ball. It is then necessary to readjust the body's whole position to return to the proper downward movement. The player *must* keep her eyes fixed on the ball until she has completed the follow-through. And always take a full swing, with a complete turn of the shoulders. In fact, it's so complete, it's really a full circle.

I'm emphasizing swing in such detail for two reasons, although one is really a part of the other. When a long-shafted club is involved, the swing is the most important element, since it is only by executing a perfect swing that the player will get full distance. Now, the drive is a distance shot and it also sets the psychological tone for the entire game. A golfer, therefore, must swing and swing well! Too many women have the idea that they must start this most important of movements by jerking the right hip back. When this happens, they find they have brought the club too far in toward the body and thereby shortened the swing. This you must *never* do on a drive. Learn to take the club back and always keep in mind that it is the left side and left hand that will do this. The right hand is just to give the left support.

I think another difficult detail for women to master is the position of the hands at the top of the swing. Since so many women are right-handed, it seems awkward to rely so heavily on the left and yet this must be. At the top of the player's swing, the knuckles of the left hand should face upward—to the sky. To achieve this, the left arm should turn at the shoulder so that arm and club are one unit, and when the clubhead is resting on the ground, the elbow appears to be locked.

If a player tries swinging the club with the left arm only, she will find it impossibe to get any control unless the left hand is placed on top of the club. If the palm is facing upward when the club is in rest

position, it can be noted that the wrist has broken before the swing is even started. When the right hand is removed from the grip, the club's pressure should be felt on the left thumb. Try it! With the left hand in this position, it is easier to *feel* the proper swing—that is, downward, with the back of the left hand leading.

Take the backswing with some feeling for the body movements to come. Get the hands set at the top of the swing and keep the wrists cocked. As the club falls to the waist, start to grip the shaft more tightly to prepare for the impact and follow-through. Follow-through should be a single smooth motion, flowing as though all of the body's joints had just been lubricated.

If the grip is tense, the body will be tense and the movements will be jerky. Then all will be lost at the start. Too much power in the right hand will close the face of the driver and the player will therefore lose her power. The shot will be smothered or hooked.

Again, too many women have the clubface closed as they address the ball and close it even more as they begin to swing through. They can come up with some really odd shots this way. It can happen that a player will have the club closed at the address and still wind up with a good shot, but in cases of this kind the swing has unconsciously been readjusted somewhere along the line so that the ball can be met squarely.

This may be the point to bring up the rhythm of the swing. Too many aspiring golfers whip the club back and swing through in one impossible attempt to hit the ball. A swing is a one-two movement. Everything goes back in one movement and forward in a second one. If a player attempts to hit in one movement, she will find herself rising on her toes and then cutting across the line of flight—and producing a dreadful slice. If, instead, the golfer relaxes as she starts the swing, so that the left heel rises slightly and turns on the first backward movement, the right knee will follow the swing through. This sets the whole body up to help the hands maintain rhythm. Failure to do this only produces an awkward chop which jerks the player up on her toes and stiffens the knees.

Oddly enough, the fact that I learned the hula before I took up golf has helped me with all of the points I've talked about in the last several paragraphs.

It may help a player who is not Hawaiian, however, if she tries to picture the perfect swing in slow motion. This little tip has always been another of my golf keys. The swing should really be taken part by part and learned that way. To be sure, the final objective is to hit the ball, but we have to know how to swing the club first and if we swing it back properly, it will follow through properly. Nine times out of ten, "thinking" the right movements, with a positive attitude, will help the player get results.

Now, why do we tee the ball up and how high should it sit? The ball is teed so that it lines up with the inside of the left heel at address. Since the face of the driver is a pretty straight one, the ball is teed so that perhaps half of it shows above the clubhead. At this height, the average player will feel (at least at first) that she can't escape skying the ball. But she can. Her movements and the arc of the clubhead will see to that.

As I've indicated, I firmly believe that to bring off a good drive, a good swing is *the* basic necessity and must be executed in that smooth, one-two motion I've been stressing. A proper swing toward the hole on your drive, ladies, and you can't go wrong.

The Practice Tee:
The Drive—Jackie Pung

It's all a matter of that one-two swing

JACKIE PUNG:
I always take a few practice swings. It helps

102   *me loosen up, mentally and physically.*

*When the club is on its way back, I'm
starting to think of the movements to come.*

*At this point, my wrists are cocked,
my left side firm but flexible.*

My hands are in the correct position, the knuckles of the left pointing toward the sky.

The weight shift is beginning here. I'm hitting into that left side.

The ball is off, but this is no time for the head to go off too. The eyes must remain on the spot where the ball was.

*All the strength has been in the left hand
and arm; the right is doing the steering.*

*Concentration is still important.
The second movement of the one-two
swing is just as important as the first, if
not more so.*

*Now the weight has shifted completely
to the left. Notice how much the flexibility
through the knees has helped me.*

*And here's end of the backswing. A
complete follow-through is the third ingredient
necessary for a good drive. The formula
is swing, footwork, and follow-through.*

Now, you take a few practice swings, Kelly, to
warm up even before you start off. I think
every player should. So swing away.
PUPIL:
Are my feet too far apart?
No, no—just have them as wide as the shoulders.

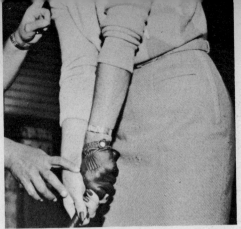

Your grip is fine. Get your left hand over, so that the "V" to the right shoulder is very plain, and get that right hand over so that your grip will have the proper firmness. Remember—emphasize pressure with the last three fingers of the left hand. The ring and middle fingers of the right hand are your pressure points.

Keep your left arm firm, Kelly. Always make sure it's nice and straight because that's your guidepost. Take it back and forth—and relax that right elbow!

Is that better?

Yes, much better. Always keep in mind, too, Kelly, that the left side is your golf side, so whenever you swing, swing left to left. Now hit a few for me.

About this far back, Jackie?
Well, for a half-swing, Kelly, you only take it waist-high, so it follows that on a drive it goes all the way back.

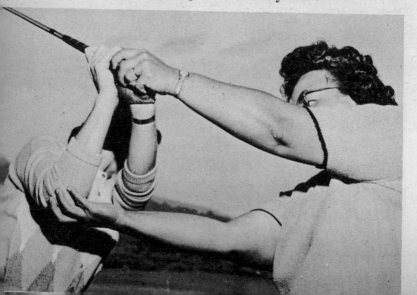

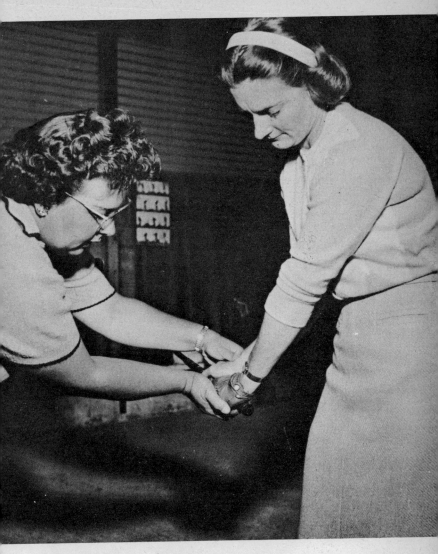

Is this any better?
Yes, it is, but keep that left arm good and
firm. You'll need it to point the shot. So
come on—let's get that left in there.
Remember, Kelly, left, left. Always leading
with your left side.

Is that too much body, Jackie?
No. If anything, it's not quite enough. You
need pivot here, so when you're using the
driver, you've got to use body. Many of us use
body all of the time. If it's a nice short
little shot, use the hands and wrists—and
footwork. But with the driver, you need everything going for you. Why don't you hit a few
shots for us? Now don't fall back, Kelly. We
can't fall back. You've got to go with it.
Go with that right knee toward the hole.

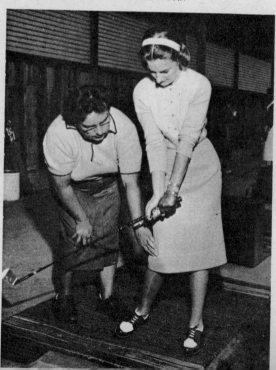

*That shot was very good, but always go through
to the finish. Always finish your shot. And
keep thinking, "left, left." Keep that left
arm nice and firm; keep your mind on the last
three fingers. Always go right through the
ball with the shot.*

That last was a good one.
But I collapsed a little, Jackie.
*A little. Now, when you collapse, it means
you haven't kept your eye on the ball. Never
take your eye away from that spot.*

113

Always feel relaxed. You can't afford any tension in here, Kelly. You must follow yourself right through. Take it up a little; grip a little shorter. Stand back a little further and reach for it—just a bit. Use your hands, but start using them right at the shoulders. Come through. Don't hold anything back.

114

Keep your eye on that ball. Always let
your hands and your right side lead you
right toward your target—but the strength,
the power is from the left. Remember, we've
got a big factor here, Kelly—timing. Right?
One and two, one and two.
One and two, right!

So—Keep in Mind:

1. STRENGTH IN YOUR LEFT HAND IS VITAL TO USING THE DRIVER WELL.

2. AVOID A FLAT-FOOTED STANCE AT ALL COSTS. YOUR WEIGHT SHOULD BE FORWARD, TOWARD THE INSTEPS, TO ALLOW FOR THE EXTREME SHIFT FROM RIGHT TO LEFT.

3. THE HEAD MUST *NOT* BOB UP.

4. THE RIGHT HAND MERELY SUPPORTS THE LEFT.

5. THE LEFT HAND IS PLACED ON TOP OF THE CLUB SHAFT, PALM DOWN, WHEN TAKING THE GRIP.

6. THE SWING IS A ONE-TWO MOVEMENT.

7. THE BALL IS TEED UP SO THAT HALF OF IT SHOWS ABOVE THE CLUBHEAD.

8. TAKE YOUR BACKSWING WITH SOME THOUGHT FOR THE MOVEMENTS TO COME.

Chapter 7

The Approach by Marlene Bauer Hagge

Mastering these shots will lower your handicap

• *Marlene Bauer Hagge was the child prodigy of golf. Today, she is one of the better known women on the links. Small (5′2″), dainty (122 pounds), she makes whaling a ball some 200 yards down the fairway seem a perfectly natural thing to do.*

To run down a list of her wins is like a catalogue of the available prizes in women's golf. The Sea Island Open, the Babe Zaharias Open, the LPGA championship, the Triangle Round Robin, the Sanford Open, the Athlete of the Year Award (1949, when Marlene was 15)—these are truly only a few of the trophies Mrs. Hagge has picked up along the way. In addition, she set an all-time money winning record of $20,285 in 1956.

Mr. and Mrs. Bob Hagge are at home in Del Ray Beach, Florida. Among her fellow professionals, Marlene has an awesome reputation as a girl who can come from out of nowhere to take a tournament. A careful study of her techniques in the following chapter will explain why.

117

• With the approach shot—and this term includes the pitch, chip, and run-up—the golfer comes to the heart of the short game. These shots are important to every player, but it is imperative that they be played well by women. And here again, achievement is based, first, on learning the proper fundamentals and then on practicing these until they have truly become second nature.

For the pitch shot, the stance should be a little wide, the left foot drawn slightly back from the intended line of flight and the ball placed approximately off the heel of the right foot. This gives the player a fairly upright position, which she will need to make the downward swing that will connect with the ball first and the turf afterward.

This last point—that the ball be hit a descending blow—is perhaps the most important element in any of the approach shots, for only this motion will give it the backspin that means control, which is an absolute necessity at short distances from the green.

The hands should be placed slightly ahead of the clubhead at address, the weight distributed equally or over to the left. As with every other golf shot, the approach needs a strong left side to hit into.

On this shot, I use either a nine or an 11 iron. When the shot is a short one, anywhere from 30 yards on in, I prefer the 11, but there are some definite don'ts in connection with this club. I've noticed that when a club with any definite loft is involved, most women tend to scoop the ball. This is dangerous anywhere; it can be fatal on an approach shot. Scooping will *not* get the ball into the air, let alone get it into the air for any distance. And another warning: those women who do not try to scoop the ball very

118

often hood, or close, their clubface. Obviously, this error is just as severe as scooping, since it dissipates the loft intended for that particular club and necessary to the pitch shot. I usually address the ball with a slightly open clubface, which helps give the club its proper loft and I keep it slightly open coming through the shot, with a very firm hand action, which means both hands working as a unit.

The golfer must always remember that the approach shot—and here we're specifically talking about the pitch—is one that is hit to the pin with a lot of backspin, so that the ball will bite. Too many golfers take a fairly long backswing and then baby the shot coming through. The correct way, the only way, is to take a short backswing and remain firm throughout the swing. To this end, the swing must be initiated with the left shoulder and arm. The club is never picked up—no jerky movement, please—it is always swung, rhythmically. It helps with the approach if the player keeps her right elbow close to her side; in other words, practically stationary. From the start of the backswing, the work should be done almost entirely by the left side, and the wrists are cocked when the clubhead is approximately a foot away from the ball.

It is extremely important *not* to pick up the club with the right hand. If the player is guilty of this seemingly easy out, she will find her hands working against each other. The downswing, too, is work for the left side. That right hand comes into play only at the point of impact. The player's left shoulder and arm actually pull the right elbow and the right hand into position so that the wrists uncock correctly and are fully uncocked at point of impact.

For myself, I find one other thing a help. I usually

take the clubhead back a little bit on the outside and then hit across the intended line of flight. This gives me a slight cut shot and, consequently, a little extra bite on the ball.

Now, for the run-up shot. Most players like it. I do and I know, too, that it can be an easy shot; just give it the proper attention. It's particularly handy if the distance between the edge of the green and the pin is short and the green doesn't hold well. In a case like this, it obviously would be impractical to use a lofted approach. Instead, the player should try hitting the ball onto the green so that it will check or stop by the pin, which is what a successful run-up will do.

This approach can be made in either of two ways. The first involves a less-lofted club like the five, six, or seven iron and the ball is hit in much the same way as a putt. The ball is approximately centered in the stance, the line of the shoulders to clubhead is straight, and the swing is pendulum-like. Here, the center of the pendulum would be the shoulders, with very little wrist action involved, so that the ball is almost parallel to the ground when in flight. The second method of dealing with the run-up requires a club with a little more loft and, in this instance, it is permissible and even desirable to hood the face slightly. This is the run-up I prefer, since it affords more control. Here, I usually use either the seven or eight iron.

I place the ball off the heel of my right foot, with my hands slightly ahead of the club at address. I start the club back with the left shoulder and arm and keep the clubhead low and close to the ground. The ball is hit with a descending blow—sharply enough so that I take a small divot. All these elements—the more lofted club, a slight hood to the face, and the descending blow—give a little more spin to the ball. Consequently, the player can pitch the ball farther, with less run on it. I feel that the more I can keep the ball in the air, the less chance I have of being defeated by the natural defects of the course: an unexpected bump, a small patch of rough, or another player's divot. In any case, the air *is* much smoother than the ground, so that the farther the ball travels through air and the more spin the player can get on her ball, the more successful the run-up shot.

I will say this, however. The golfer's choice of run-up shot must be the one with which she feels more comfortable, the one in which she has more confidence. Confidence is probably ninety per cent of a woman's golf game (really, of anyone's golf game), and since this means that golf is mental, it follows that if the player uses the shot she's happiest with, that shot is the one that will come off for her.

The chip—perhaps the most important of the approaches—is used for any shot from one to five feet off the green. It is important to keep the ball low to the ground, and you need to get some run on it. A seven, eight, or nine iron is used, depending on the length the player has to carry over the edge of the green. Normally, I use an eight for a chip. The stance here is slightly open, with the left foot drawn a little back from the intended line of flight, the ball placed off the heel of the right foot. The player's weight should be on the left side and it remains there throughout the shot. As in the pitch and run-up, all movement—the downswing as well as the backswing—is initiated by that left shoulder and arm.

With the eight iron, the clubface is hooded slightly at address, while the hands are ahead of

the clubhead. The right elbow is kept close to the right side. For the chip shot, I grip the club down quite a bit farther than I do with the other approaches and I bend more at the waist. The grip itself, while firm, particularly at impact, should be an easy one. That is, you're not gripping the club to death. Here again, the ball is hit a descending blow by the hooded face to give it backspin. This extra control makes it easier to judge the distance and that is possibly the most important factor in chipping.

The last important thing the player must remember on the chip shot is the terrain she's playing. If she is going downhill to the hole, the best method is the one I've just described—that is, a slightly hooded eight iron hit a descending blow. If the chip is uphill to the pin, I would go to a less-lofted club, like the six or seven, hooding the face a trifle, but hitting the ball with a more side-powered blow, not quite the descending shot the downhill position requires. This is so that the arc will be a little flatter. And there should still be backspin on the ball.

To generalize on all of the approach shots: keep the shoulders, arms, and hands flexible. Aside from these focal points, there is very little body movement involved. It's a question of control. And to repeat, exercising control requires confidence. Really, a woman's golf game is such a psychological thing that it sometimes defies description. I've played with my husband often enough to know just how psychological it is. I know from the women I play with just how psychological it is. Because approach shots are crucial to her short game, the woman golfer's tension as the green gets closer is worse than the man's. But if a woman lets panic take over on the approach, she's lost.

This short game is the part of golf that women should and must concentrate on, because it is the part of golf in which they can excel. A woman who can keep the ball in play on the other shots, while chipping and putting well, will be up there with the best of them. I should know because I'm a small girl. If it weren't for these areas of my game, I wouldn't have a chance. And another thing: I've trained myself to leave a bad hole behind me. Forget it. There's absolutely no point in letting one three-over-par destroy an entire game. I stop thinking about it as soon as I've left the hole. Even when it's hard to do, I force myself to think of the next shot; it *could* set me up for a birdie!

Golf has been an important part of my life since I was twelve. I've thought a lot about it and I've come to the conclusion that what goes on in the head is as important, say, as the muscles that are used to power the two iron. First of all, we've acknowledged that golf is a psychological game. Second, it's a game of judgment. Knowing what club to use when. Knowing when to power a shot and when to play it safe. Knowing when to pitch and when to chip. A woman's judgment (sometimes mistakenly called intuition) is generally very sound, so she's one up there. Third, golf needs a sure sense of touch, of depth perception, and it's been proved over and over again that here women *are* the sure sex. With all of these elements going for them, it should be obvious that the fact that a man's ability to outdrive his lady love is not going to affect their score cards appreciably. After all, it's the total that makes the game. And it's a woman's short game—her approach—that decides the total. On that basis, it's almost easy to feel sorry for the male animal—but not very.

The Practice Tee:
The Approach—Marlene Bauer Hagge

A student refines her pitch, chip and run-up

MARLENE HAGGE:
The most important things to keep in mind on this
shot are hand position and keeping those hands
firm at impact. On an approach shot like this
(editor's note: the ball was approximately 45 yards
from the pin), *you can either pitch the ball or*
run it up, whichever is most comfortable for you.
PUPIL:
From here, I usually try to pitch it.
That's a fine shot if you use it well. Now, I feel that
placement of the ball should be about two inches off
the heel of the right foot. This will allow you to hit
the ball a descending blow and give it backspin.

However, I would have you move the left hand over a little more.

To the right? That feels uncomfortable.

Well, anything new will feel uncomfortable at first, but try it and see how it works for you. Also, I'd try gripping down a little farther on the club. Now, why don't you hit a few? Hit to the green and I'll see what your swing is like.

I missed that one by a mile!

Well, you see, you took too long a backswing. The swing should be very firm, but short and compact. And I'd grip down even farther on the club. This is a short shot, so we don't need a full swing for it and, as a result, we can grip the club shorter. Another thing: you tend to scoop the ball and shorten that grip still more. Get the ball back more toward the right heel. You're taking the club back on the inside, Peggy, and for this shot that's not good. Take it back on the outside and cut slightly across the ball coming through so that you get more backspin.

Remember to keep down on the shaft so that there is about two inches of the grip showing. Also, bend a little more at the waist and bring your left shoulder forward a bit, because throughout your entire swing —on both the short shots and the long shots—the left shoulder and side should always be leading. Bend slightly at the knees. Now, feel that you are going slightly on the outside of the line with the ball rather than on the inside.

That last shot of mine was very poor.
**Well, you took a divot with that one at least—you
contacted the ball first and took the turf afterwards,
which is the way all of the iron shots should be hit.
But you're still taking the club back on the inside
and so you scoop the ball most of the time. You
should feel as though you're taking the club back
high and coming down directly on top of the ball.
And one last point: cock your wrists a little more.**   127

Marlene, I just can't get my direction right.
You had the face closed in this manner, rather than
keeping it straight. The line from the toe of the
club to the grip should be a straight line. Maybe
if I demonstrate a little bit, it will help.

Now another thing: on the backswing, here is
where the wrists should break up. And you can only
do that by going back on a straight line or slightly
on the outside. Your last shot was O.K. You were
just afraid of what was going to happen on contact
with the ball and you're still taking too long a
backswing. You are coming back up to here which
is almost a three-quarter nine-iron shot. If you
think of breaking your wrists a little bit sooner
going back, it will shorten up that backswing.

I'm still going in the wrong direction,
though—and I'm trying your suggestions.
That's because you're still pulling the ball coming
through. You're hooding the club a little and trying
to scoop it; "steering," in other words. Just let it
alone. But you notice that the ball is biting better
and staying by the hole. Just remember that if you
break your wrists a little sooner, it will shorten up
the backswing, and then you'll hit down on the ball.

Now, this particular shot is called the run-up shot. It's used anywhere from 20 yards on in. It comes in particularly handy when the distance between the edge of the green and the pin is short and the green doesn't hold well. On the shot, we usually use a six or seven iron. Notice that I've placed the ball off the heel of the right foot, with my weight on the left leg and foot. I have my hands forward, ahead of the ball, and I drag the shot coming through, keeping the hands very low throughout the swing. On the run-up, the ball is still hit with a descending blow.

*Bring the club straight back on the line. Start it
back with the left side; the left arm swinging the
club back . . . that's better, only coming through.
Don't try to hack it. You're getting turf first. Come
down on top of the ball. Try not to hit the right
hand into it too much.*

That last one was no good at all.

*You're rushing the swing now. Before you've
finished your backswing, you're trying to scoop it
through on the downswing. Your swing must be
well-timed—a one-two movement. And you're
rolling your right hand over coming through.*

There! That's better. Your left side should initiate
the backswing and the downswing as well. But you
did roll that right hand over at the last minute,
sending the ball to the left. Remember, straight
on through.

It would be so easy to get discouraged!

Try not to, Peggy. Your stance is nice and open now,
although the ball could be back farther, and closer
to the right heel. And you've got your hands ahead
nicely, though you don't have the weight enough
to the left even yet. Lean toward the left and
concentrate on that hand doing the work, rather
than helping it with the right.

This next is what we call the chip shot. For this shot, most people prefer the seven or eight iron since the ball has to run quite a distance—for about four feet off the edge of the green. Normally, I use the eight for this shot. It doesn't really matter; the best iron is the one you're most familiar with. Note that I'm standing quite a way ahead of the ball; the stance is open and the ball is just off the right foot. My hands are slightly ahead of the ball so that the clubface is hooded just a little to keep the ball low and give it a bit more run.

I take the club back on the swing with the left side initiating the movement as it does with the downswing. Although a divot is not taken on this shot, the ball is still hit with a descending blow. The backswing should take the club back right on the line and through. Here, position—both of the hands and the feet—is extremely important.

That's fine. Take a shorter backswing, however, and be a little firmer coming through the ball . . . Very good. Remember, now, to keep the weight over on the left through the shoulders, too. On that last one, you picked up a bit with the right hand; it was steered coming through. I can't say too often: the swing must be initiated with the left arm and the left shoulder to prevent scooping. Besides, scooping it will pull the ball to the left. Keep the club going through down on the ball.

*Should there be much body movement in
a shot like this?*

**No. Most of your movement should be from the
shoulders. That's the center of your arc and
everything begins there. Other than that, the body
movement is very slight. Now, the body should be
leaning a little forward, and again, the weight is
over to your left. You have one problem, Peggy:
you're inclined to raise up on the left and let the
right side lever it through . . . that's better!**

Too many times, players will take a long backswing and then baby the shot coming through. You should shorten the backswing and be firm. That last one was fine, although you pulled it just slightly. You were a little bit afraid of it. Just keep the club coming down through the ball, through the shot and through the line . . . Good! You can even be a little shorter on that backswing of yours. Remember: descending blow, no scooping, short backswing, weight on the left, and firmness at impact. Keep these in mind and your chip shot will do just what you want it to do.

So—Keep in Mind:

1. THE MOST IMPORTANT FACTOR IN THE APPROACH SHOT IS THAT THE BALL BE HIT A DESCENDING BLOW.

2. THE APPROACH NEEDS A STRONG LEFT SIDE TO HIT INTO.

3. ON PITCH SHOTS, ADDRESS THE BALL WITH A SLIGHTLY OPEN CLUBFACE.

4. ON ALL APPROACH SHOTS, KEEP THE BACKSWING SHORT, REMAIN FIRM ALL THE WAY THROUGH.

5. THE BACKSWING AND DOWNSWING BOTH MUST BE INITIATED WITH THE LEFT SHOULDER AND ARM.

6. NEVER PICK UP THE CLUB WITH THE RIGHT HAND. IF YOU DO, YOU WILL FIND YOUR HANDS WORKING AGAINST EACH OTHER.

7. THE RIGHT HAND COMES INTO PLAY *ONLY* AT THE POINT OF IMPACT.

8. TAKE THE CLUBHEAD BACK A BIT ON THE OUTSIDE; THEN HIT ACROSS THE INTENDED LINE OF FLIGHT.

9. REMEMBER: THE AIR IS SMOOTHER THAN THE GROUND. THE FARTHER THE BALL CAN BE MADE TO TRAVEL THROUGH THE AIR, THE MORE SUCCESSFUL THE RUN-UP.

10. THERE IS LITTLE BODY MOVEMENT INVOLVED IN THE APPROACH SHOT. CONTROL IS WHAT YOU'RE AFTER AND THIS STEMS FROM THE SHOULDERS.

11. KEEP IN MIND THAT EVERY PLAYER GETS MORE TENSE AS THE DISTANCE TO THE PIN DECREASES; DON'T PANIC.

12. AS LONG AS YOU CAN KEEP THE BALL IN PLAY ON YOUR OTHER SHOTS, AND CAN CHIP AND PUTT WELL, YOU WILL PLAY A GOOD GAME OF GOLF.

Chapter 8

Trap Shots
by Louise Suggs

If you can swing a club, you can hit out of a trap

• *In 1951, Louise Suggs was elected to Golf's Hall of Fame. This was not extraordinary in the light of her achievements; it was exceptional since she had won her first competition only ten years before.*

Since 1941, she has taken the Women's Southern twice, the Titleholders' four times, the Western Open four times, the Women's International Four-Ball, the U.S. Women's Amateur, the British Ladies' Amateur, the All-American Open three times, the Women's National Open twice, the Cross Country Weathervane, the St. Louis, Pan-American, Oklahoma and Eastern Opens, and the Triangle Round Robin, (this last twice), the Havana Women's Invitational, the LPGA championship, the Heart of America Open, the Babe Zaharias Open, the Gatlinburg Open, the French Lick Open, the American Women's Open, the Links Invitational, and the Vare Trophy.

The new professional at Castleview, a 36-hole course in Atlanta, Louise Suggs brings to her teaching the same brilliance she has shown in competition.

• Trap shots are really among the easiest shots in golf. The thing that makes them so terrifying is the fact that the trap is a natural hazard, and golfers are just not set up psychologically to accept hazards without some element of panic. The average player also makes the mistake of feeling that she must help the ball up and on its way. The only way a trap shot can be played successfully is to play it as you would any other shot—with ease and concentration, the basic elements of stance and swing modified to a degree, but only a degree.

Now, the major difference between trap shots and any others in golf is the fact that the trap shot requires that you hit sand *first* and then take the ball. Generally speaking, I hit the sand about an inch to an inch-and-a-half behind the ball. You see, it is the sand, more than the loft of the club, that gets the ball out of the trap. And it is the sand that gives the ball as much backspin as you can get on a trap shot. However, before I expound on this, let's look at the clubs you have to work with.

For my trap shots, I use a double-service niblick, but that's because I have so many clubs in my bag that I haven't got room for more than one wedge, and the niblick I'm talking about is fine for certain fairway shots as well as the traps. This allows me to stay within the 14-club limit imposed by the U.S.G.A. The sand wedge, with its wide sole, will also do the job and, there are some people who prefer the 11 iron, which has more loft than the nine, not quite so wide a sole as the wedge and is not quite as heavy. I personally feel that the niblick I use, and the wedge, are designed for heavy duty and will get you out of any kind of sand, whereas the 11 will sometimes require a substitute, but here again, it's a question of the individual golfer's preference.

The major reason for my choice, beyond the confining limits of the 14-club maximum, is that the double-service niblick eliminates the necessity for changing clubs when I encounter different qualities of sand. Obviously, there are not only different grades of sand, but different consistencies within the same grade, depending on the weather—powder sand can turn into something like either glue or granite, depending on the amount of rain the course has had. This means that your stance varies, depending on the distance you hit behind the ball, which depends on the kind of sand you're dealing with. The lighter the sand, the farther behind the ball you can hit and the more open the stance. Conversely, in heavy sand or gravel, you must square your stance slightly and hit directly behind the ball. Here, it is absolutely impossible to give accurate directions in terms of inches away from the ball, or the degrees to which the stance is opened in specific situations. These combinations are intangibles that the golfer comes to through experience rather than instruction.

The first thing to remember when you've landed in a trap is that, since the trap *is* a hazard, it's against the rules to ground your club. You must hold the clubhead slightly above the sand and you must not touch it on the backswing, nor are you allowed to pick up pebbles, leaves, sticks, or any other debris that may have found its way into the trap. The penalty for either of these misdemeanors is two strokes. This doesn't mean, however, that you can't remove man-made objects. They include soda bottles, cigarettes, and other trash. Unfortunately, you may *not*

obliterate someone else's footprints. In other words, if you've had the misfortune to land in the print of the golfer who played through before you, you'll have to grin and bear it. But you might keep in mind that, rather than engender the same rage in someone else that you feel as you swing and hope for the best, you should, you *must* erase your own footprints as you leave the trap.

The stance for an ordinary trap shot is an open one with the left foot pulled away from the line of flight so that the player's body is almost facing the target. You should also be sure that your stance is a firm one—with the feet planted in the sand rather than on top of it. The ball is played well forward, off the instep of the left foot. This open stance automatically makes the golfer take the club outside of the line of flight. I personally feel that I'm swinging it out—perhaps pushing it is a better description—with the left hand. Here again, the left hand and side lead. My grip is the usual overlapping one I use for all my shots except putting. Remember, the trap shot is played like any other. But if fluidity, or smoothness, is important at any time during the game, it is absolutely essential here. This is one time when you can't afford even a small twitch, because that would cause the club to hit into the sand and hang there just as though it were hung on the root of a tree. So, swinging back down smoothly, I cut right across the ball, which also helps throw it up in the air. I do *not* open the face of the club. That would give me a tendency to shank the ball, so I keep the blade square throughout the shot. I also feel that by hitting it slowly and deliberately, I use my hands and wrists a lot which means that I can flip the ball if it's sitting cleanly in the sand—or on top of it, to put it another way.

If the ball has hit soft sand with a decisive plop, it will usually be buried and create what I call a well, or a depression, in the sand. I try to hit the edge of that depression. When a ball is in this position, it won't have much backspin and you must make allowance for that, too. You'd have to be enormously strong to get through enough of the deep and soft sand to give it backspin, but lacking that, I just allow for the ball to run a little farther on the green. I don't even try to hit it as far as I would if it were sitting on top of the sand.

Another instance in which the player needn't hit the ball with quite as much authority is when it is on the uphill side of the trap. Then the ball will fly up suddenly anyway, since the blow will be coming up under it. In this situation, you should have the feeling that you are floating the ball out. Here again, your left hand leads. You take the sand first, and the ball will sail up a bit after that. Obviously, the follow-through on this shot will not be a complete one (your hands will pass the ball, but just that) since your body is already off balance and an attempt to follow through normally would send you sprawling.

If the ball is on the downslope, or the backside of a trap, it will be a difficult shot. The only advice I can give here is to make up your mind that it will be a tough one and be philosophic about it. Hit it as well as you can and don't panic! This is about *the* most difficult shot in golf, but since you will not be able to hit it perfectly every time (no one can!), there's no point in worrying about it. Just go into it. Use an even more open stance. Now here, I don't mean "wider,"—I mean "more open"; in other words, the body is faced even more markedly toward the hole. Take the club outside of the line of flight more than you have with the other trap shots and actually flip it. You've heard people say that they've used a flipped wedge, for instance. When I say "flip," I mean use your hands and wrists to flick the club, but very slowly. However, the actual picking up of the club is a little more abrupt, so that you do get sand first, but not as much. As a matter of fact, ideally, you'll get sand and the ball at about the same time. Just try to pick the ball off the sand as cleanly as you can; as I said, not quite so much sand behind it—and you're out. There will be no full follow-through in the usual sense here, either. Again, your precarious position and the fact that you're grounded on sand will allow only for the clubhead and hands actually to get through the ball.

Trap shots are never fun, but if you leave fear behind, you can manage them so that you're within putting distance. As with every other situation in golf, it's the fear that will do you in. A trap is, after all, simply another part of the fairway's contour. It's a deeper part, to be sure, and the material you're hitting from is different. But—if you've practiced your trap shots, if you remember that the sand is actually there to help you, if you refuse to panic, landing in a trap will be an occasion for a mild, lady-like expletive and not a signal for nine holes of gloom. As a matter of fact, I'd rather hit from a trap than a tight lie on the fairway. It may help to remember that in picking a ball from the sand cleanly and quickly, delicacy is an important factor. Perception is another. And women have more of both. So play your trap shot and smile.

The Practice Tee:
Trap Shots—Louise Suggs

Every golfer needs to know that sand is her ally

LOUISE SUGGS:
Remember, Erma, that the most important thing in a
sand trap is that the sand helps to lift the ball into
the air. You don't have to try to raise it. Use an
open stance and set your hands well ahead.
PUPIL:
I don't really understand the reason for that.
Well, it's simply to set up a strong left side. This is
especially important for trap shots.

*You know that you can't ground your club in a trap.
Now, I'm going to mark a spot here and I want you
to watch—and instead of aiming at the ball, aim
at that spot and swing very slowly and deliberately.*

*But before you swing at the ball, be sure your stance
is open, that is, your left foot is drawn back away
from the line of flight. And when you swing, push
the club away from the ball, outside the line of
flight. On the downswing, return in the same arc
so that you cut across the ball intentionally.*

146

*I think it's because I'm so nervous when I land
in a trap that I have so much trouble.
I'm sure that's it. The physical elements of
trap shots—the movements you've got to remember
to make—are really simple. It's what goes on in
your mind that can throw you! Now here, your
left foot could be drawn back farther. This open
stance is very important, because it helps limit your
backswing and it gets your body out of the way
more quickly on the downswing.*

**One thing you have a tendency to do, Erma, is to
scoop the ball. Never try scooping or lifting it—
just play it forward with an open stance and hit the
sand first. The swing itself, if you take it through
to the finish, will get the ball into the air.**

147

*Your movement at the end of the swing
seems so much quicker, Louise.*

**Well, the only way to get out of the trap is to make
sure the ball rises quickly, so all your action is
through your hands and wrists. Always start the
clubhead away from the ball outside the line of
flight. Do this intentionally, so it will be a cut shot
and that will get the flick you need.**

**Notice that when you're coming through on a trap
shot that the wrists are very limber. But there is
a definite flipping effect. And the follow-through is
a complete one—not as full as you would have on
a long iron or a wood shot, but then the arc you're
describing isn't as full, either. But if you want to get
any bite on the ball at all, besides lifting it up and
out, watch the follow-through. It must be complete.**

148

So—Keep in Mind:

1. A TRAP IS A HAZARD IN WHICH YOU MAY *NOT* GROUND YOUR CLUB.

2. THE SAND CAN BE AN ALLY. HIT INTO IT BEHIND THE BALL AND SO USE IT TO PUT MORE BACKSPIN ON YOUR SHOT.

3. USE AN OPEN STANCE IN A TRAP. IF YOUR BALL IS UP AGAINST A STEEP BANK, USE AN *EXTREME* OPEN STANCE.

4. THE BLADE MUST HIT THE SAND SQUARELY.

5. SHORTEN UP ON YOUR BACKSWING.

6. ON A TRAP SHOT, PICK THE CLUB UP MORE ABRUPTLY AS YOU GO INTO YOUR FOLLOW-THROUGH. USE A DEFINITE FLICKING MOTION WITH THE HANDS AND WRISTS.

7. BE DELIBERATE ABOUT THE SHOT IN ORDER TO ACHIEVE FLUIDITY.

8. CONCENTRATE ON MASTERING THE SAND CLUB YOU PREFER TO USE; LEAVE THE QUACK THEORIES ALONE.

9. THE LIGHTER THE SAND, THE FARTHER BEHIND THE BALL YOU CAN HIT AND THE MORE OPEN THE STANCE. CONVERSELY, IN HEAVY SAND OR GRAVEL, YOU MUST SQUARE YOUR STANCE SLIGHTLY AND HIT DIRECTLY BEHIND THE BALL.

Chapter 9

Trouble Shots
by Marlene Bauer Hagge

Trouble shots are only trouble if you think so

• Trouble shots are so special that most of this chapter will be made up of photographs taken of specific situations—the most frequently recurring trouble spots in which I've found myself.

As with everything else, however, there are a few generalizations that can be made about those moments when a player comes face to face with the fact that she is in a spot where getting her par is virtually impossible.

Of all the factors involved in these trouble shots, judgment is probably the most important—and the most difficult. The golfer must decide whether to gamble and go for the green in one tough shot that could, however, land her in even hotter water, or whether to play it safe and take the extra stroke right off the bat.

I always advise a player—as does every professional I know—to play the percentages. For instance, if you're doing extremely well, you're relaxed, so take a chance. If you need par badly, that's the time to take the extra stroke, since the tension you're under anyway would probably make the gamble shot a bad one. Sometimes, playing it safe is hard to do, but invariably, it pays off. Bev Hanson once said about percentages, "I always like to play the shot that makes the next one easy. Golf is a game of percentages; if you stick with the house percentage, you're in business." Bev knew what she was talking about.

It isn't that I can't pinpoint dozens of trouble shots; it's that I'd rather not think about most of them. However, if you want a few shudders, you might consider these:

You may find yourself on a sandy road, dotted with pebbles. Your choice of a club would depend on the consistency of the material from which you're hitting. But then, how far from the green are you? If I were 150 yards from the green, I'd probably take a four iron and just try to get the ball back to the fairway. The only flat statement I could make about a situation like this is that I'd *never* use a wood; it would ruin the club.

Or, you could find yourself in thick woods. In this situation, if the boughs of the trees are low-slung, I'd take a two iron and chip the ball onto the fairway. In a case where the trunks of the trees are crammed together, I'd scream "unplayable lie" and take stroke and distance. Unless, of course, I could help myself more by dropping directly behind the unplayable position and play it from there. And take the one-stroke penalty. Percentage, remember.

Or, the ball has lodged in the broad root of a tree. What's behind you? And how far away from the green are you? I play a shot like this with anything that comes to hand, if I think it will give me a chance to get out.

Or, you've landed on hardpan. If you're within 135 or 140 yards of the pin, you might make it with the five wood, hitting the ball first and more or less bouncing it off the surface.

Or, the ball is in a position where you have to play it with your left hand—for instance, it's smack up against a stone wall or fence. I'd take a three or four iron, turned on the toe, and simply try to get the ball out. I couldn't take a chance on ruining my putter.

Now you see why I say that every trouble shot is a game in itself. The emergency measures you take when you get into trouble can't be dreamed up ahead of time; they are simply consistent with common sense and quick thinking, used when trouble is what you're in at the moment. If you ask Louise Suggs how to play out of an equipment house off the fairway, she'll tell you to get the grounds keeper to move the mowing machine first and then take your two iron. She couldn't have told you before it happened. Every professional I know tries not to think about trouble before they're in it, and then the money-makers play the percentages.

I've been playing golf for a very long time and I can still get panicky when I find myself in a tough lie. This is something that I fight constantly to control, since it is the panic, not the lie, that defeats the player. No matter how repetitious it may become, how tedious to listen to over and over again, it cannot be emphasized too strongly that golf is a game of mind over matter. The psychological approach, particularly for women, determines, nine times out of nine, the score card's total. And nothing can undermine confidence more than indecision. Naturally, I think that my suggestions regarding percentages are good ones—they work for me. But the most important element in exercising the judgment involved with those percentages is making a decision and sticking with it. Look over the spot you're in. Take your time, but don't dawdle, either. Then decide what you're going to do and try to bring it off. If it works, you're out in front. If it doesn't, it still won't have proved conclusively that you were wrong and, after all, it is the next shot that is always the most important.

This is a typical trouble shot: trees. One near the ball cramps the swing. Another stands between me and the green.
I can either play it safe and chip back to the fairway, with the certain loss of a stroke, or I can gamble and go for the green. What club, what execution? My choice: a) an 11 iron, hit with an open stance, quick hand-cocking on the backswing, and hitting down through to carry the 75 yards high over the tree in front of me, or b) hooding a less-lofted iron and hitting to the green with a slight hook to carry under and around the green slightly to the left.

I'll first play the shot over the tree with the eleven iron.
I place the ball forward of the center of a slightly open stance.
I'll open the clubface and swing the club through with
early timing—that is, quickly bringing the hands up high
on the follow-through. Playing the shot over the tree is
slightly more exhausting and there is more margin for
error, but if it comes off, there's more of a chance that I'm
close to the pin.

It worked. The ball went right over the tree and is within
fifteen yards of the pin. The lie for this shot is tricky since
there's no grass at all—just bare dirt. How do I do it?
Hit on through as though there were turf.

Now I'll play the ball the other way—under and around the tree between me and the green—with a six iron. As I said, the green is 75 yards away and I'll try to hit under the tree, hooking it a little. On this shot, I will take the ball back—off the heel of my right foot.

Here, it's necessary that I keep a very firm left arm throughout the swing. I'll hood the club slightly at the address and continue to do that as I come through the shot so I get my hook. And to insure this, I will pull my right hand over a little. Also, the weight distribution will be mainly on the left side.

Now here, I am square up against a tree. As you can see, it's impossible for me to take any backswing at all. The only way I can head the ball toward the green is to aim for the tree itself so that the ball rebounds from the trunk. That will move it toward the green and the hole for a short distance, at least. For this shot, I'll hit the ball just as I would a full nine iron—but remember . . .

To use the nine iron, you need that full swing to hit the ball into the tree hard enough so that it will rebound. And with the nine, you'd have to hood the clubface a little bit. An alternate choice would be to use a less-lofted club and aim with the fairly straight face. Well, I got out—about six feet —and at least it's now in a playable position.

. . . *One thing we haven't discussed in connection with trouble shots is the consideration a player must give the wind. Say you have 150 yards to go to the green—and to further complicate matters, a tree is directly in the line of flight. Here again, we have a choice—to slice around the tree, hitting from left to right, or we could hook around the obstacle, going from right to left. A situation like this really calls for a careful evaluation of the wind. If it's blowing from right to left, I'd hit a hook. But if the wind is going from left to right, I would slice—and let the wind help me. If, on the other hand, there is no wind to speak of, then the player must use the shot in which she has the most confidence.*

Now. If I'm hooking, I'll use the four iron and place the ball slightly to the right of center of my stance; that is, between my right foot and center. The stance is slightly closed, the right foot drawn back a little from the intended line of flight. On this shot, the club is brought back on the inside of the line and the player should roll the hands a bit coming through.

To slice the ball around the tree, the stance is again a moderately open one, with the left foot drawn back, the ball slightly forward of center in the stance. The club comes back on the outside of the line and cuts across the ball coming through. Actually, the swing is an outside-in swing. Here, I'd delay the hand action a little and leave the clubface open at impact. This gives the ball a little more of what we call left-to-right English and helps the slice.

Talking about the wind may give you some idea of the consideration you've got to give the intangibles, whether you're playing a straight shot or one commonly called a "trouble shot." That's why it's so difficult to lay down any specific rules for trouble shots; the number of variables can be staggering! For instance, another point is the selection of a particular club. This is a problem that is never really solved, but in the trouble category, the factors involved in making a decision are even more numerous. Here again, it's a matter of common sense; simply use the club that you feel will give you the edge.

When we come to the five wood, I'd have to say that we women professionals consider it the handiest club in the bag. Since it has the distance of a two iron and the loft of a five, it's a great club if you want to hit the ball high into the green and have it bite—that is, make the ball stay rather than run. This wood has no peer when it comes to getting the ball out of a fairway divot, or high rough, and it's fine for a bare lie. The first shot I'll demonstrate is one in which I've got to get out of a fairly bad fairway divot.

The next shot I'm going to demonstrate with the five wood is one off bare dirt. There's no grass, so no point in trying either to scoop the ball or to get it up in the air. Remember—that with all the fairway woods, although you do not take a divot, you still hit the ball a descending blow, since you're not teed up. Now for the five wood off a bad lie on the fairway with absolutely no grass underneath.

The five wood is the club I normally use to get the ball out of the rough. With this shot, it is still very important to remember that the ball be hit a descending blow. Never *try* to scoop it. You must also keep in mind that when you are in a spot like this, the grass tends to swing the clubface closed at contact. To compensate, therefore, you must address the ball with the club open a bit—this will help battle the grass as it tries closing the face.

In the pictures on the opposite page, all you're going to see, really, is a swing—and that's all there is to shooting over a water hazard. It so happens that on this shot, I'm about 130 yards from the pin—and about forty of those yards are water, but I'm thinking only about where the ball is supposed to go and not about where it could go if something goes wrong. That is the secret of water hazards. A player doesn't ordinarily give much thought to the kind of fairway that is between her and the hole (I'm not talking now about what may be off to the left or right)—she's trying to make straight yardage. And that depends on smoothness and good timing. Forget everything that might *happen* when you run into a water hole; look at the pin and see only that. Make the swing a one-two movement—smoothly—and don't ever try to rush. It's undeniably true that the more uncertain you are, the faster you'll swing. and a speedy backswing only throws your head up and ruins your entire effort. Like almost everything else in golf, a water hazard is no problem if you can keep cool. Panic is every golfer's worst enemy; if it can be defeated, the game is all but won.

Chapter 10

Putting
by Louise Suggs

A putt is the stroke that makes every woman a pro

• The ability to putt well is a vital necessity for any golfer, but since it is the decisive element in the short game, it assumes even more importance for women. Let those who can do it belt the ball down the fairway. *You* practice those green shots; they'll save more strokes in the long run than adding an extra twenty yards to your drive.

For women, the putt is psychologically difficult for two reasons. First, the prospect of finally getting the ball into the cup usually makes the player more tense than any other point in the game. But this applies to men as well as to women. The second reason is clearly marked "For women only." Holing the shot is, after all, the climax of the short game and it is this game that the weaker sex must concentrate on if golf is to be more than a pastime. In fact, if a woman is to consider herself a golfer at all, she must be a demon when it comes to saving shots on the approach and putt. Now that we've established the fact that there *is* a psychological hazard connected with canning the ball, I can say flatly that it is only this hazard that makes the putt difficult at all. The confident player will sink about 50 per cent more putts than the woman who allows herself to give way to the jitters. Along with trap and trouble shots, the "power of positive thinking" is an absolute necessity for this part of the game.

First of all, I think of the putt as a miniature of my regular swing. By doing this, I can avoid the danger of bringing the club back on the outside— something that frequently happens if the golfer is concentrating on a short backswing. To take the grip first, I use the reverse of my regular overlapping grip; that is, instead of having the pinky of my right hand resting on top of the left index finger, the left index finger rests on top of the right pinky. This limits the manipulation of the hands and wrists—something that is very important in a motion that is circumscribed anyway. I keep my hands at least even, or slightly ahead of the ball, so that my left hand leads all the way and sets up a strong left side. This should give you the feeling that you're almost pushing the club toward the right toe on the backswing. I use a square stance, with both toes on the line of flight and play the ball off the left foot.

Now, in stroking through the ball, I get the feeling that I'm hitting toward the hole with the back of the left hand. It's not really steering; it's more like aiming a gun. Here, the individual golfer's own idiosyncrasies come in, for I personally don't feel that the swing for a putt is a pendulum swing—that would make me feel as though I were about to sway off the ball—fall away from it.

Another trick of mine is to flex my elbows just enough, with the top of the clubshaft drawn in toward me, so that my right elbow is resting on my right hip bone. Not the side of the right hip, mind you—the hip bone itself. This position makes it difficult for me to pick the club up with the right hand, which would send it outside the line of flight. In that sense, it's really a form of protection against a dangerous putting fault. On all golf shots, it is important that the player be comfortable; putting is no exception. Bending easily at the waist is not only the correct and comfortable way, but it also gets your head in the proper position. This brings up a point that most professionals can become bugs on—or at least, I can. *You must keep your head steady*. Now, keeping your head steady doesn't mean necessarily that your eyes must be fastened on the ball every second of the time. It means that your eyes must be directly *over* the ball and your head must remain in that position. We know that the blind can play golf, so it isn't a question of seeing the ball, it's simply that if you keep your head over it, you won't sway off your target.

Another of the problems a player will run into on the putt is determining the relationship between the length of the putt and the degree of strength with which she must hit the ball. There can be no rule of thumb on this at all. It's a matter of feel. After you've been batting the ball around the green for a while, you'll be able to feel just how hard you must hit the shot. One tip that might help you is my method of looking over the green. If you've ever seen me play, or putt, you may have noticed that I don't crouch to survey the green. Instead, when I've addressed the ball, I swivel my head, while my body remains in address position, so that it's facing the hole, and eye the ball squarely—never with a side-long glance. It must be the perspective, but it makes it much easier to ferret out the unexpected breaks and hollows that my ball will meet on its way to the cup. Finally, when I try for the hole, I have a mental picture of a larger one in my mind—one that is about four feet in diameter. If you aim for that four-foot hole, you'll be pleasantly surprised, I think, at the number of putts you'll sink.

When it comes to uphill and downhill putts, as well as breaks on the green (or sidehill putts), you must remember that putting is basically the same all the way. It's a matter of touch and that old standby, confidence. Both of those come only through experience. However, I know that when I'm hitting uphill, into the grain, I hit a little more firmly. I have the feeling of popping it—slapping it, sort of, with the back of my left hand.

On a downhill lie, if the green is slick, you can lag it—tap it gently—again with the left hand. Whichever way you can do it successfully will be the best way, of course, but this is my method, and the only way I can describe it. It still seems to me to be the simplest because it helps my putts and it's a complete backstroke in terms of the arc required by the shot. When you take the club back, you can hit it hard or you can hit it easy, but it must stay in the groove. *If* you've made the putt the miniature of your regular golf swing.

For sidehill putts how much you'd allow for breaks depends on whether you're a cut putter or a hook putter. I happen to be a hook putter and if the break goes from right to left, I have to allow more than the cut putter. By the same token, if the break goes the other way, I don't allow as much. Finally, the speed of the green determines how much it will break. You'll always have a sharper turn on a slick or fast green than you'll get from heavy grass.

Probably one of the game's best putters is Dr. Cary Middlecoff, and his recommendations bear out what we've already said—that golf is a highly individual game. For instance, Cary suggests that you survey your putt in two different ways: from the side and then from directly behind the ball. He is also pretty emphatic in saying that once you've done this, go ahead and make the shot without giving yourself any time for indecision. Another thing Dr. Middlecoff points out is that if you concentrate on the kind of grass in the three-or-four-foot circle around the hole this can help you determine the amount of strength you will have to put into the putt. For instance, if the grass is rough and thick, then you can really take a good whack at it; if it's smooth, lag your shot. Try his method; it may be right for you.

In reading back over this, to hole a putt on paper sounds terribly uncomplicated—and since I know the frustration and sheer rage that can go into a putt, it hardly seems fair. But putting *is* easy if you can relax. I suppose I sound as though I thought anyone could hit in the low seventies consistently if they lived on tranquilizers. Well, if it's not quite as easy as that, it comes close. Golfing, to repeat my favorite theme, is a question of learning the rudiments and then practicing them until they've become a part of you, but your attitude toward this learning and playing is perhaps more important than anything else. If I do sound like the needle's stuck, it's only because this recognition of the role the mind plays in golf is a lesson that all pros learn in time. And with putting, I can truly say, "It's all in your head."

The Practice Tee:
Putting — Louise Suggs

A golfer drops an elbow, holes a ball

LOUISE SUGGS:
As you know, putting is mainly a matter of confidence, Jane. It's not so much a matter of doing a thing in a certain way as it is making up your mind that what you are doing will get that ball into the cup. Now to me, the most important thing in the putting stroke is the grip.

167

PUPIL:
Isn't my usual grip all right, Louise?
**Well, your usual grip is the normal one—a regular
overlapping grip and it's fine. However, I've found
that the best grip for me is a reverse overlap—like
this. Just reverse the pinky of the right hand and the
left hand's index finger. The only other time I might
use this is on an approach when I need a lot of run.**

**Now, I'm going to try not to change your natural
style of putting more than I have to. When you line
up toward the hole, you are playing the ball off your
left toe, which is fine because that keeps the ball
up forward, and gives you more overspin on it.**

A putting stroke to me, Janie, has always been like a miniature of my regular swing. Just bring the club-head back, straight away from the ball and then go toward the hole on the follow-through. That's the only way you want the ball to go. Now, of course, there are many different ways of doing the same thing in golf—that's where those individual differences come in. I may do it a little differently because I have more confidence in my way than in any other. You must do whatever you feel works out best for you. Also, when you're standing over the ball like this, just be relaxed—feel that you're bending in order to get over the ball and that you're in complete control.

Do you bend your knees on the putt, Louise?
**Not particularly, and I don't recommend it since
it can make the player squat and she'll fall away
from the ball.**
*What do you mean by being over it? And how
close do I get?*
**Well, I'm not as close as you are and I feel
comfortable when I'm about six or eight inches away
from it. That's it. Now just lean over it. That's the
idea. You see—that gives you a little more balance
and control.**

**Now your stance should be practically square. Don't
get the ball outside the left foot. I always try to be
certain that the hands are at least even to slightly
ahead of the ball, so that you have some overspin on
it when you come through. When you take the putter
back this time, Jane, try to remember my idea that the
putt is a miniature of your big swing. Well, in a big
swing you turn away from the ball—here, just try
to swing away inside as you would on a regular shot.**

*The big point is not to get discouraged. Sometime,
I'd like to see you drop your arms toward your body
a little more. Just try it.*

It seems to work a little better.

*Well, the reason for that is that if your arms stand
too far away from your body, you have a tendency
to pick up the putter. As a matter of fact, I rest
my right elbow on my right hip and that prevents
my picking up the club.*

What about the left arm?

*Just let it drop naturally. It doesn't have to rest
against the body—just let it swing smoothly. You
should have a feeling that you're taking the club
away with both hands. There you go.*

*Technically, when you try to take that club straight
away from the ball, you lift up—plus the fact that
you actually get outside of the line of flight. Try to
swing it inside a bit. The ball will go a little truer
for you.*

Do I break my wrists?

**Yes. When you take the putter back, you should have
the feeling that you are bringing it in this direction—
more or less as though you were swinging it
toward your right toe and your wrists break a little
when you get halfway back toward your toe.**

Is the weight distributed equally?

**More or less, but if there is any difference, it should
be slightly on the left foot. Keep the ball forward off
the left toe. Back away from it a little, so that
you're comfortable.**

*I'm not sure I understand the business about
bending over the ball, Louise.*

**I said just to bend forward a little as naturally and
normally as you can—from the waist—so that
you're comfortable. Don't be stiff or try to stand up
straight—just let your knees bend backward as we
call it. I feel that most women are slightly double-
jointed, or at least more flexible in the joints than
men are as a rule, so that bracing the knees
slightly doesn't inhibit their movements as much
as it does a man's.**

One other thing, Janie. Remember that a woman's height usually prevents her from accomplishing much if she bends her knees. If she bends her knees, she probably will squat and fall away from the ball.

So—Keep in Mind:

1. IN NO OTHER PHASE OF THE GAME IS CONFIDENT RELAXATION SO IMPORTANT.

2. TRY THINKING OF THE PUTT AS A MINIATURE SWING.

3. TO KEEP THE CLUB BLADE CLOSE TO THE GROUND AND AVOID "PICKING UP" ON THE BALL, TRY A REVERSE OVERLAP GRIP; THAT IS, THE LEFT INDEX FINGER OVERLAPS THE RIGHT PINKY.

4. THE HANDS SHOULD BE SLIGHTLY AHEAD OF THE CLUBHEAD.

5. THE PUTTING STANCE IS A SQUARE ONE AND THE BALL IS PLAYED OFF THE LEFT TOE.

6. THE RIGHT ELBOW SHOULD REST COMFORTABLY ON THE RIGHT HIPBONE: THE LEFT ARM HANGS EASILY — FREELY.

7. YOU MUST KEEP THE HEAD STEADY. ANY JERKY MOVEMENT CAN RUIN A PUTT.

8. VISUALIZE THE CUP AS THE CENTER OF A LARGER AREA AND AIM FOR THIS.

9. A FAST, OR SLICK, GREEN GIVES THE BALL MORE OF A BREAK.

10. AN UPHILL PUTT REQUIRES A LITTLE MORE FIRMNESS, WHEREAS YOU CAN TAP A DOWNHILL PUTT. BUT IN BOTH CASES, YOU SHOULD FEEL AS THOUGH YOU WERE HITTING WITH THE BACK OF YOUR LEFT HAND.

Chapter 11

The Golf Clinic

*The game's top women professionals
answer questions most often asked by players—
their initials identify the answering pros*

• **When can I start to play golf—out on the course?**
I think after a minimum of ten lessons. You'll have begun
to assimilate the swing and be more confident. You'll also
have learned good course etiquette. (B.R.)

• **What do I do when I get a bad lie?**
Just be calm and try to get out of it the best way you can.
Don't try for a spectacular recovery. Try to hit into position
for a good chip and a putt. (B.R.)

• **How can I gauge my distance better?**
Get to know the feel in your hands. Your eyes will tell your
brain how long the shot is, but you have to get the feel of
the distance in your hands. (J.P.)

• **How far away from the green can I be and still
use my wedge?**
That depends on how far you can hit it! To insure accuracy,
though, I think not over 80 yards. (L.S.)

• **What do I do with my feet?**
Don't think about them. Keep your balance during the
swing and just let your feet work naturally. (J.Z.)

- **I play tennis well—why can't I play golf?**

You can. If you can play tennis well, you have the necessary co-ordination. Remember, tension is your enemy in golf and the key word is "relax." (R.J.)

- **Why is it called the driver?**

Because it's the club used to drive off the tees. In the same way, the number one iron is the driving iron. All clubs used to be called by name, not number. (L.S.)

- **What are the lines on the club face for?**

They give the ball a grab, so that it doesn't slide off the face when hit. They also serve as a guide, so that you can get the club face square at address. (J.P.)

- **Am I stupid in learning so slowly?**

The inability to learn golf quickly and easily shouldn't jar your confidence in your intelligence. Remember that the so-called "natural swinger" is one in a million. All of us had to learn, just as you will. Compare learning golf to taking a course in calculus without benefit of basic mathematics. Golf is different from almost any sport or exercise you may already know. But you can and will learn to play golf, as millions of enthusiasts are proving every day. (B.H.)

- **When will I get the ball in the air?**

You'll get it up when you hit down on it. (R.J.)

- **How high do I lift my arms?**

You should *swing* to a position natural and comfortable for you. If you think of lifting your arms to a specific height, you'll be working your whole body, and each time you'll have trouble getting the club into the proper position. (J.Z.)

- **Why do I top the ball?**

This is usually a result of a golfer's futile attempt to assist the club in getting the ball into the air. Just the opposite happens. Rather than keeping your hip, shoulder, and knee levels fairly constant through the hitting area, you probably raise your entire body. Your weight is then well up on your toes, your head and shoulders are jerked out of position, and if you hit the ball at all, it'll be with the bottom of the club and the shot will have no loft to it. (B.H.)

• How much time should I put in on practice?

That depends on what you want from golf. Remember, a potential champion must work much harder than someone who just wants to play well enough to join her husband on Sundays. No matter how much time you spend, be particular about aiming your practice shots at a specific target. Don't hit aimlessly. Don't spend hours working on just one club. Work on shots of different length, with the emphasis on your weak clubs. Don't practice too long at one time. Two 30-minute sessions are better for you than one hour. (B.H.)

• What is the U.S.G.A.?

The United States Golf Association is the governing body for amateur golf (and for all practical purposes, professional golf, too) in this country. It establishes golf rules, maintains a greenskeeping section, and promotes such tournaments as the U.S.G.A. Men's Amateur Championship, U.S.G.A. Women's Amateur, junior championships for boys and girls under 18, a Public Links Championship for men, and the U.S.G.A. Opens for pros. (B.H.)

• How many lessons do I need?

It's a matter of your own pace in absorbing what your pro is trying to teach you. The fundamentals are the most important, and until they have really become habit, you should continue with lessons. (M.H.)

• How fast should I swing?

The tempo with which a golfer swings is one of the important factors in successful golf and varies from player to player, since personality helps determine a golfer's best speed. Some of us are cut out to be slow swingers, others fast—but good swingers are always consistent within their own tempo. (B.H.)

• What do you do when you're in a slump?

I'm afraid you have to live with it. A slump is the result of being overgolfed, or the underlining of a basic fault. I mean that a golfer can go for a fairly long period with an incorrect swing, stance, or grip, but the time comes when this fault is so aggravated that the player's entire game suffers. Try to get a pro for at least one lesson. She can diagnose the fault and make suggestions. From there on, it's a question of practice. If a player is "overgolfed," however, the only solution is to curl up with the latest *Vogue* and refuse to think about the game. It's the panic that defeats you. This is just as true of a slump as it is of a trouble shot. (L.S.)

• Am I too old to start to learn golf?

I like to think a woman is too old to start golf only if her heart has stopped beating. While it's true that people lose some co-ordination with age, I think it's possible to place too much emphasis on youth. One of the strongest recommendations for golf is that it's one sport in which older people can participate. (B.H.)

• What kind of equipment do I need to begin?

Your equipment should be prescribed and fitted by your professional instructor—and only by her. (M.H.)

• What is a chip shot?

A chip shot is neither pitched nor rolled, but a moderate combination of the two. It's usually used on the aprons of, or approaches to putting greens. (M.H.)

• Do I have to count a "gimme" putt as another stroke?

You certainly do. The rules of the game say that you have to count each stroke, given or not. (B.R.)

• **Why do I have to overlap my fingers when I take my grip?**

You don't have to, but those who have played for a long time feel that it tends to give a better, firmer grip. Your hands won't be as likely to slip. (L.S.)

• **How high should I tee the ball with an iron? With a wood?**

You should generally tee the ball an inch from the ground for irons and a fraction more for woods. (B.R.)

• **What do you mean by "cocking your hands?"**

This really means cocking your wrists, which is exactly like cocking a gun. In a good swing, your wrist breaks properly at the top of the backswing, setting up the hands so that they can be released through the hitting area. This cocking gives the clubhead the speed necessary to propel the ball into flight. (M.H.)

• **Why do I do so much better when my instructor is watching?**

Usually you're concentrating on what she's telling you, and you have a terrific desire to show her how quickly you respond. Concentration is directly connected with hitting the ball well. (B.R.)

• **How far do I stand from the ball?**

Stand as close as you have to to allow for a proper swing. If you stand too far away, you'll be reaching and are likely to be thrown off balance. (R.J.)

• **Why can't I use my wrists?**

As far as I'm concerned, you can and should. They can help you generate more clubhead speed. (L.S.)

• **Why should I let my swing follow through to the right when I want the ball to go straight?**

As a matter of fact, the follow-through should not go to the right, but straight ahead. Golfers used to be taught to move their forward swing from inside to outside—or right. This move blocks the golfer through the hitting area and restricts the proper release of the clubhead. Golfers are now encouraged to move their forward swing from inside to straight ahead. (B.H.)

● **Why should I start my turn first?**
You shouldn't. You ought to start your swing at exactly the same time that you start your turn. (R.J.)

● **How can I turn my hips without turning my shoulders?**
The question isn't how can you, but why would you want to? The more tensile strength a golfer can build up in her shoulders, the more power she can bring into play. I know many top golfers who use a swing based on a minimum of hip turn or pivot, but I don't know any top golfers with a swing based on no shoulder turn. To function ideally, the shoulders and hips must turn at the same time and work in unison. (B.H.)

● **Why am I hooking and why am I slicing?**
If you hooked, you probably rolled your hands and wrists over at the moment of impact, and had a closed stance. If you sliced, you probably fell away from the ball. A slice is the result of cutting across with the hands and wrists coming through the ball. (L.S.)

● **Why should the ball be placed off the left heel?**
It doesn't necessarily have to be played that way. You should place the ball at the low point of your swing. I've found that it's never placed farther back than center, or farther forward than the instep of your left foot. Playing the ball off the left heel seems to be the happy medium between the two. (J.Z.)

● **How do I get distance?**
Intelligent practice is a potential source of distance, as you

179

will firm up the muscles in the hands, forearms, back, and legs, and you will learn to know and trust your swing. When a player feels she's swinging well, she instinctively swings with real authority, thereby generating that extra spark of clubhead speed that means solid, powerful contact with the ball—plus, inevitably, added distance. (B.H.)

• **Why do I seem to lose power before I hit the ball?**
The chances are that you're "hitting from the top." Most long-ball hitters try to hold back their right hand and forearm power until they are almost back to the ball. One way to do this is to make sure that, at the top of the backswing, your right elbow points toward the ground. This position seems automatically to curtail the desire to hit from the top. (B.H.)

• **Why do I have trouble hitting to an elevated green?**
You shouldn't. Just trust your swing and the club and don't try to push the shot in the air. (J.Z.)

• **How do I get backspin on the ball?**
Hit through the ball with a descending blow. A good axiom to follow is ball first and turf afterward. (B.R.)

• **Why can't I use my wedge, just off the green?**
Because it's usually too soft and delicate a shot for the loft of the wedge. Any slight malfunction of your swing will result in your hitting too far behind or under the ball, or hitting too high. It's much safer and easier to use a five, six, seven, or eight iron and hit a relaxed pitch-and-run shot. (M.H.)

• **What makes me look up?**
It could be hitting at the ball too hard, falling away, or anxiety about your shot. (L.S.)

• **How can I get out of a steep trap?**
You should generally play the ball well forward and with an open stance. (L.S.)

• **Is it permissible to use a sand wedge when I'm not in a sand trap?**

Yes, definitely. The wedge can be used on the fairway when you need to put extra spin on a chip shot. It's also a valuable scoring weapon from the fringe rough around the green. The weight of the club helps you get the ball out of the coarse grass. (B.R.)

• **When putting, how can I tell if the ball will roll to the right or the left?**

The ball will break away from the high side and roll to the low. You will need practice and experience to be able to judge how much it's going to roll. (J.Z.)

• **Why do I putt so badly?**

You probably don't have enough confidence in the way you're doing it now. Use another method and cheer up. Don't get too tense and don't try to force it. (L.S.)

• **Why don't I get the same "feel" every time I hit an approach shot?**

Because "feel" comes from crisp, correctly executed shots, which in turn come from a correct swing. The chances are you're not swinging properly. (M.H.)

• **How can I keep my head still?**

By pointing your chin at your right toe and leaving it there until you have contacted the ball. (M.H.)

• **Do you get many off-beat questions during a clinic?**

Most questions during a lesson or a clinic are pretty standard. However, one unusual and amusing incident occurred with a young woman who had had a few lessons before and was being given specific instruction on her irons. I asked her to take the club in her hands, set her stance, and address the ball in preparation for the swing. She took the proper grip, placed her feet in position, looked down at the ball, and quite seriously and blandly said, "Hello, Ball!" (R.J.)

181

Chapter 12

Clothes for the Course
by Louise Suggs

Clothes and equipment can make a woman both pretty and comfortable

• We've come a long way from the days when the only outfit allowed a woman golfer was a shirtwaist and hobble skirt. The final touch to this costume was a straw boater—and that sat on top of a pompadour that must have quivered with every swing and quaked in every fairway breeze.

Finally, however, the men saw the light and allowed as how it might not be too distracting if women were to wear shorts, as long as these were tailored to hit just above the knees. And so—we've been liberated.

This is not to say that there are no rules at all when it comes to the kind of clothes a woman should wear on the course, but most of these are really a question of common sense and good taste.

The first prerequisite for anything to wear while playing golf is that it fit properly. Golf, after all, requires a number of sweeping gestures. A top that doesn't fit properly can inhibit a swing just as surely as the wrong shoulder movement. A badly cut, ill-fitting pair of shorts can ruin a putt as easily as an interfering pebble. If the player is as comfortable as possible, her game will be improved immeasurably.

Comfort doesn't mean, however, that any woman must look as though she had just been to a rummage sale at an Army-Navy supply store. Manufacturers have kept weather eyes peeled during the last few years as women have taken to the greens in increasing

numbers, and the selection available now, while not as extensive as some might wish, is certainly varied, attractive, and remarkably inexpensive.

The clothes on these pages, for example, are simple but smart, the shorts and tops tailored for action. Besides their classic simplicity, their colors and fabrics mark them good-looking and up-to-date. The dresses are not for the course proper, unless you feel more comfortable in dresses than you do in the more informal garb, but they will sail through marketing, chauffering, and the on-display kind of day that includes lunch at the club with no fuss. It's completely up to the woman involved.

Shoes, for golfers especially, are of prime importance. Here again, the current models are beginning to reflect women's demand for chic. The first thing I'd have to advise a player to look for, however, is the proper fit. It's bad enough to suffer agony for an evening or a day of intermittent walking in ill-fitting shoes. A round of golf requires several hours of foot movement. Need I say more?

I've saved the most important note of this chapter for last. And it isn't properly fashion, inasmuch as it concerns equipment, although the colors of the bags and the designs for the hoods for clubs are now aimed specifically at women and range from light 184 blue, to white, to combinations. The clubs, of course,

MEMBERS
MUST REGISTER
GOLF GUESTS
AT PRO SHOP
BEFORE PLAY...

are woman-tailored. They're lighter and shorter, among other things, and they constitute the major investment a player makes. A not inconsiderable investment, either, but it is worth every penny. It *is* possible to learn the rudiments of golf with a man's clubs, but it is inadvisable. There are those who are rabid on the subject of beginning lessons with one's own clubs, since any flaw in address, or grip, or swing is hard to correct later on, and it stands to reason that when a player switches from one set of clubs to another some inches shorter, it will affect her game.

There are all sorts of gimmicks, gadgets, and addenda to the fashion story. Individuality has more or less centered on hats and bags, and there are any number of these designed to elicit smiles and/or compliments. The more prudent of the merchandising fraternity have also caused a number of rain jackets, umbrellas, and rain slacks to be made for the hardy souls who care less about the weather than breaking a hundred. Golf bags may be player-toted in a variety of lightweight carts. One can see from all this that except for the clubs themselves, the cost of golfing paraphernalia is strictly up to the player. The question of fashion on the course might be summed up by three axioms: clubs must fit, clothes should be comfortable, and dramatic effect is more often achieved by a swing than a sweater.

185

Chapter 13

The Rules and
Etiquette of Golf

A discussion of two of golf's greatest problems—
what you may do and what you should do

ABOUT THE RULES

Often the most misunderstood aspect of golf is the question
of rules. The only official rules are issued by the United
States Golf Association and the Royal and Ancient Golf Club
of St. Andrews, Scotland. Here is a simplified guide to some
of the more important.

TEEING OFF

When you are driving from the tee, the ball must be
teed up between the markers and not more than two club-
lengths behind the markers—never in front of them. If the
ball falls off the tee before you've taken your forward swing,
you may replace it without penalty. But if you swing and
miss the ball, that's a "whiff" and it counts one stroke.
If you "top" the ball, that counts as a stroke, and you must
play it as it lies.

MOVING BALL ACCIDENTALLY

If the ball (not on the tee) moves accidentally while you are
addressing it, you must count a penalty stroke and play it
as it lies.

The information in this chapter is used by permission of the United
States Golf Association and is based upon the Rules of Golf, copy-
right by the United States Golf Association 1951, 1953, 1954, 1955,
1956, 1957, 1958, 1959.

BAD LIE

If you improve your lie by moving, breaking or bending growing vegetation, except incidentally when taking a fair stance or when swinging, you lose the hole in match play. In stroke play, the penalty is two strokes. But outside of hazards you can move loose natural impediments like tree branches, fallen leaves or loose stones, although if you move the ball in doing so the penalty is one stroke (no penalty on putting green). Moving loose impediments is not permissible in hazards except when leaves cover the ball. Hazards are bunkers or sand traps, bodies of water, any water course, ditches.

ORDER OF PLAY

After the tee shots, the player whose ball lies farthest from the hole plays first.

MOVING OPPONENT'S BALL

In match play, an *opponent* must take a penalty stroke if he, his caddie or his clubs touch or move a player's ball. This penalty does not hold in stroke play. The player must *place* the ball on the spot from which it was moved.

In match play singles, there is no penalty if a player's ball moves the opponent's ball. The opponent may play the ball as it lies or place it on the spot from which it was moved. The same holds true in stroke play except when both balls lie on the putting green or within 20 yards of the hole, and neither ball is in a hazard; in the latter case, a two-stroke penalty must be taken.

USING THE WRONG BALL

If you play a stroke or strokes with a ball other than your own except in a hazard, you lose the hole in match play or are penalized two strokes in stroke play. There is no penalty if you play the wrong ball in a hazard, provided you then play your ball.

DROPPING THE BALL

Whenever the ball must be dropped in accordance with the

Rules of Golf, you must face the hole, stand erect and drop the ball behind you over your shoulder. If you fail to do it in this manner and the ball remains in play, you must take a one-stroke penalty. If the ball rolls into a hazard, or out of bounds, or more than two club-lengths from the point of dropping, it may be re-dropped without penalty; if it rolls nearer the hole than the point of dropping, it must be re-dropped.

LOST BALL

A ball is "lost" if it cannot be found within five minutes after you or your caddie begin to search for it. Signal any players behind you to "go through" while you look for your ball. If you can't find it, you must go back to the spot from which you played it and play another, counting all strokes actually made (U.S.G.A. trial rule for 1960). If the lost ball was played from the tee, it may be re-teed. Otherwise it must be dropped. If your ball is found after you have played another, you must take the penalty and continue to play the second ball.

BALL OUT OF BOUNDS

If your ball goes out of bounds, you must go back to the spot from which you hit it and play another, counting all strokes actually made (U.S.G.A. trial rule for 1960). For example, your first tee shot goes out of bounds. When you hit again, you are shooting two.

UNPLAYABLE LIE

If your ball lies against a tree or in some other similarly bad spot, you yourself must decide whether you can play it from there or not. If you decide it's playable, you must play it as it lies. But if you decide it isn't, you may go back to the spot from which you hit it and play a ball, adding one penalty stroke to your score for that hole. Or, under a one-stroke penalty, you may drop a ball so as to keep the point where the first ball lay unplayable between you and the hole, and play it from there (but in a bunker the ball must be dropped in the bunker). You may go back as far as you like in dropping a ball.

OBSTRUCTIONS, GROUND UNDER REPAIR, CASUAL WATER

If your ball touches a movable artificial obstruction, such as a hose, you may remove the obstruction. If your ball lies on or touches some immovable artificial obstruction, like a bench or drinking fountain, you may drop the ball within two club-lengths of the nearest point on the outside of the obstruction, but not nearer the hole. You are entitled to the same relief if the obstruction interferes with the stroke or the stance. If, anywhere on the course except in a hazard or on a putting green, your ball lies in or touches casual water or ground under repair or a hole made by a burrowing animal, you may, without penalty, pick the ball up and drop it behind you, no nearer the hole but as close as you can to the spot from which it was lifted, on ground which avoids the specific bad condition.

If, *in a hazard,* your ball lies in casual water, ground under repair, or in an animal hole, you have a choice of playing it as it lies or lifting it and dropping it in the hazard as near as possible to the spot where the first ball lay but not nearer the hole, so as to get the most relief possible from the bad condition. Under penalty of one stroke, you may lift it and drop it outside of the hazard as near as possible to the spot where the ball lay but not nearer the hole, keeping the hazard between you and the hole.

If your ball is "lost" under any of the conditions described, you may drop a ball without penalty as near as possible to the place where the ball last crossed the margin of the area, not nearer the hole.

On the green, if your ball is in casual water, ground under repair or in a hole made by a burrowing animal, or if such conditions lie between your ball and the hole, you may lift the ball and place it in the nearest position to get relief but no nearer the hole.

WATER, HAZARDS AND TRAPS

If your ball is covered by sand, fallen leaves or the like in a water hazard or sand trap, you may remove as much of the material as necessary so you can see the top of your ball.

There is no penalty if the ball is moved during such removal, but it must be replaced. If your ball goes into a water hazard from the tee, you may tee up another ball and take a stroke penalty in addition to the one already played. If your ball is in a water hazard and you think you can play it as it lies, you may do so. If you can't play it, instead of going back to the place you played from, you may drop a ball behind the hazard, keeping the spot where the ball last crossed the margin of the hazard between you and the hole; in this case, however, a one-stroke penalty will be incurred. If your ball lies in a lateral water hazard, another ball may be played from the spot where you played the last stroke, or you may drop a ball within two club-lengths of either side of this hazard opposite the point where the ball last crossed the hazard margin but no nearer the hole. Penalty—one stroke in either case.

If you play your ball from a water hazard or a bunker, you must not let your club touch the water or the ground until your downstroke. This applies to the exposed part of a sand trap. The grassy side of a sand trap is not considered a part of the hazard, and you *may* ground your club there.

STRIKING THE PIN

The player playing the stroke—off or on the green—has the option of deciding whether or not he wants the pin removed. There is no penalty for his ball striking the pin when it is not attended or has not been removed but he must continue to play, in his turn, until he holes the ball.

In stroke play, if your ball hits the attended pin or the player attending the pin, you must take a two-stroke penalty, regardless of the distance from which you hit the ball.

ON THE GREEN

When you reach the green, don't bring your clubs onto the green. Leave them on the side closest to the next tee, and carry only your putter.

BALL AGAINST PIN

If your ball lies against the pin, it cannot be counted as being in the cup. If, when you pull the pin out, the ball drops in, it is counted as "holed out." If the ball falls away from the pin, it may be replaced on the lip of the hole and putted in, and the strokes required to do it must be counted.

OBSTACLES ON THE GREEN

If leaves or other loose impediments lie on the green, you may remove them without penalty. If your ball moves after a loose impediment has been touched, it must be replaced and there is no penalty. You may repair ball marks on the green, provided you don't step on them. You may clean the ball on the green.

PUTTING

If another ball lies in the line of your putt in single match play, if you are the "away" player, it is your decision as to whether your opponent may or may not lift his ball. The player who picks up his ball must mark its position, preferably with a small coin, or some other thin flat marker; if the marker might interfere with your putt, it may be placed a measured distance away.

In stroke play, if a ball on the green interferes, you may require its owner to lift it or play first, at his option. If the other player thinks his ball on the green may assist you, he may play first.

In single match play, if your ball knocks your opponent's ball into the cup, he is considered to have holed out on his previous stroke.

Again, in single match play, there is no penalty for hitting your opponent's ball on the green. The other player may play the ball from its new position or put it back in the place from which it was moved.

If your opponent's ball has come to rest on the lip of the cup, you may concede the putt in match play. But in stroke play, there is no such thing as conceding a putt: every player must hole out on every hole. In stroke play, when both balls lie on the putting green or within 20 yards of the hole and neither ball is in a hazard, if you hit the other player's ball you must take a penalty of two strokes and the other player's ball must be returned to its original position.

Etiquette

1. No one should move, talk or stand close to or directly behind the ball or the hole when a player is addressing the ball or making a stroke.

2. The player who has the honor should be allowed to play before his opponent or fellow-competitor tees his ball.

3. No player should play until the players in front are out of range.

4. In the interest of all, players should play without delay.

5. Players searching for a ball should allow other players coming up to pass them; they should signal to the players following them to pass, and should not continue their play until those players have passed and are out of range.

6. Before leaving a bunker, a player should carefully fill up all holes made by him therein.

7. Through the green, a player should ensure that any turf cut or displaced by him is replaced at once and pressed down, and that, after the players have holed out, any damage to the putting green made by the ball or the player is carefully repaired.

8. Players should ensure that, when dropping bags or the flagstick, no damage is done to the putting green, and that neither they nor their caddies damage the hole by standing close to the hole or in handling the flagstick. The flagstick should be properly replaced in the hole before the players leave the putting green.

9. When the play of a hole has been completed, players should immediately leave the putting green.

PRIORITY ON THE COURSE

In the absence of special rules, singles, threesomes or foursomes should have precedence of and be entitled to pass any other kind of match. A single player has no standing, and should give way to a match of any kind.

Any match playing a whole round is entitled to pass a match playing a shorter round.

If a match fail to keep its place on the course and lose more than one clear hole on the players in front, it should allow the match following to pass.